Mountain Biking
Albuquerque

NICOLE BLOUIN

FALCON® Helena, Montan

D1042853

A FALCON GUIDE®

Falcon® Publishing is continually expanding its list of recreational guidebooks. All books include detailed descriptions, accurate maps, and all information necessary for enjoyable trips. You can order extra copies of this book and get information and prices for other Falcon® books by writing Falcon, P.O. Box 1718, Helena, Montana 59624 or calling toll free 1-800-582-2665. Also, please ask for a free copy of our current catalog. Visit our website at www.FalconOutdoors.com or contact us by e-mail at falcon@falcon.com.

©1999 by Falcon® Publishing Inc., Helena, Montana
Printed in Canada.

1 2 3 4 5 6 7 8 9 0 TP 05 04 03 02 01 00 99

Falcon and FalconGuide are registered trademarks of Falcon® Publishing Inc.

Cataloging-in-Publication Data

Blouin, Nicole, 1966-
        Mountain Biking Albuquerque / by Nicole Blouin.
            p.   cm. -- (A FalconGuide)
            Includes index.
            ISBN 1-56044-746-X (pbk.)
            1. All terrain cycling--New Mexico--Albuquerque Region Guide-
        books. 2. Bicycle Trails--New Mexico--Albuquerque Region Guide-
        books. 3. Albuquerque Region (N.M.) Guidebooks. I. Title. II.
        Series: Falcon guide.
        GV1045.5.N6A533 1999
        796.6'3'0978961--dc21   99-22407

                                                                                    CIP

CAUTION

Outdoor recreational activities are by their very nature potentially hazardous. All participants in such activities must assume responsibility for their own actions and safety. The information contained in this guidebook cannot replace sound judgment and good decision-making skills, which help reduce risk exposure, nor does the scope of this book allow for disclosure of all the potential hazards and risks involved in such activities.

Learn as much as possible about the outdoor recreational activities in which you participate, prepare for the unexpected, and be cautious. The reward will be a safer and more enjoyable experience.

 Text pages printed on recycled paper.

Contents

Acknowledgments

So many people helped with this project, but first and foremost I'd like to say thanks to Charlie Ervin and Two Wheel Drive bicycle shop. I couldn't have started, much less completed, this project without Charlie's assistance. He told me where to ride, when to go, and what to expect.

My boyfriend, Rob Edwards, explored many of the rides in this guidebook with me. His sense of adventure and his love of the sport kept me going. He never complained when we got lost *again!* Thanks also to Dawn Souza and Chrissa Constantine, my dearest friends in Santa Fe, who also accompanied me on a ride or two.

I'd like to extend a sincere thank you to several agencies around Albuquerque that support mountain biking trails: Sandia Peak Ski Area (Chris Boyden), Albuquerque Open Space (Ondrea Lindroth), and the Sandia and Mountainair Ranger Districts of Cibola National Forest.

A special thanks goes out to the trail builders and to those who continue to maintain the trails around the city. Albuquerque is lucky to have Trail Ways, an affiliate club of IMBA, to help organize the efforts of mountain bikers in the area. Please give them your support.

Just a few more thank you's: to Ace Mountain Wear and Bike in Santa Fe for tuning my bike, to Peggy O'Neill-McLeod for the careful line edit on my manuscript, and finally, to Falcon Publishing for the editing position waiting for me in Helena, Montana, as soon as I finish this project.

MAP LEGEND

～	Trail	Ⓢ	Trailhead	
～	Unimproved Road	Ⓢ	Route Marker	
～	Paved Road	🏔	Elevation/Peak	
～	Gravel Road	🏔	Volcano	
～	Interstate	(15)	Interstate	
～	Wilderness Boundary	(12)	U.S. Highway	
～	Waterway	(143)	State Highway/County Road	
	Lake/Reservoir	092	Forest Road	
	Cliff	•—•	Gate	
△	Camping	🏠	Building	
⊼	Picnic Area	•——•	Powerline	
≍	Bridge	N↑	Scale/Compass	

```
0     1     2     3
|—————|—————|—————|
        MILES
```

vi

•Albuquerque Area

TO SANTA FE

44

25

Bernalillo

165

Placitas

17

Rio Rancho

SANDIA
PUEBLO
INDIAN
RESERVATION

108-19

CIBOLA
NATIONAL
FOREST

TO
SANTA FE

22

12-13

24-25

14-16

11

Albuquerque

20

SANDIA
RANGER
DISTRICT

10

East Mountain

40

21

9

66

Tijeras

40

23

1-3

4

6-7

TO
GRANTS

KIRKLAND
AIR FORCE
BASE

DEPT. OF
DEFENSE
WITHDRAWL

8

TO
MORIARTY

ISLETA INDIAN RESERVATION

337

25

Rio Grande

9

55

Tajique

Torreon

TO
ESTANCIA

CIBOLA NATIONAL
FOREST/
MOUNTAINAIR
RANGER
DISTRICT

TO
MOUNTAINAIR

N

0   5   10

MILES

Get Ready to Crank!

Welcome to the Land of Enchantment—a landscape as diverse as its culture. Ride through volcanic mesas, juniper and pinon woodland, ponderosa pine stands, high elevation spruce/fir forest, and the Rio Grande bosque. Sound good?

Albuquerque sits in a lush river valley surrounded by dry desert country with rugged granite peaks towering over it all. It doesn't matter whether you are a beginner or an expert rider, Albuquerque has something for everyone. The 25 rides in this book represent the amazing contrasts in this distinctive part of the Southwest.

The biggest technical challenge on the singletrack around Albuquerque is rock. Some of the terrain is steep and rugged, and trails cut through canyons and across boulder fields. On many of the rides, you will encounter abrupt rock steps, or "staircases," which are particularly difficult to climb. These staircases often interrupt an otherwise awesome stretch of singletrack and can last from a couple moves to almost half a mile. When you combine this with some loose rock, things get even more interesting. If you want to see these staircases at their worst, try the Faulty Trail. You may come to love it or hate it.

The Rio Grande runs straight through the city, creating a green ribbon of life in an otherwise arid landscape. The special habitat located in the floodplain of the river is called a bosque. Here, you will find easy rides beneath the cottonwood trees. To the west of the river, dormant volcanoes line the horizon. The volcanic terraces within Petroglyph National Monument provide some fun exploring on moderate, rocky trails.

The cliffs of the Sandia Mountains rise abruptly out of the city's backyard from 6,500 to 10,678 feet. While the majestic granite spires lie within the wilderness boundary where only hikers, horseback riders, and climbers are allowed to play, the rocky foothills contain a great trail system for mountain bikers. This is the best riding right in the city.

The Sandias slope more gently down their forested, eastern side. East Mountain is often called Albuquerque's playground, although most visitors only see this beautiful area by car as they drive along New Mexico 536—Sandia Crest National Scenic Byway. As the road gradually climbs from a semi-desert to an alpine environment, you can experience the climate, plants, and animals of four different life zones including the Upper Sonoran, Transition, Canadian, and Hudsonian life zones.

King of the Mountain, a great alpine ride at the Sandia Peak Ski Area, is one of the highlights on East Mountain. The chairlift runs from Memorial Day weekend to mid-October. Hours of operation are 10 A.M. to 4 P.M., Thursday through Sunday, plus holidays. In 1998, a one-way lift ticket cost $7 and an all-day ticket cost $12. The ski area is the site of the Sandia Peak Mountain Bike Challenge, a series of five races throughout the summer. The trails open later on race days and the lift rates are discounted.

Note: The fee for parking at trailheads for most of the rides on East Mountain and the northern slope of the Sandias was

$3 per vehicle in 1998. This is an experimental user-fee program that the USDA Forest Service implemented and it looks like it is here to stay. For more information, contact Cibola National Forest.

One of the best areas for mountain biking around Albuquerque is the trail system at Cedro Peak and Otero Canyon. Don't miss this extensive network of singletrack just off Interstate 40 and south of the town of Tijeras. It includes about 15,000 acres of rolling, pinon-juniper woods. Currently, this multi-use area is visited mostly by mountain bikers and equestrians. A detailed map of Cedro Peak and Otero Canyon is available from Two Wheel Drive bicycle shop in Albuquerque or the Sandia Ranger Station in Tijeras.

How to Use This Guide

Most of the information in this book is self-explanatory. If anything in a ride description doesn't seem to make sense, read the following explanation of the format again. There is also a glossary in the back.

The 25 rides in this guide are divided into ten areas around Albuquerque. It is important to note that all of the trails under a given heading are connected in some way to one another. This gives you the opportunity to form longer loops and to create a variety of different trips.

Note: The only exception is the Foothills Trail System. While the North Foothills and the South Foothills are connected by Trail 365, the route follows the city's paved bike path along Camino del Sierra.

The maps are clean, easy-to-use navigational tools. Closed trails are not usually shown but may be listed in the ride description. Most of the information was taken from USGS topos and Forest Service maps. While each nook and cranny may not be depicted, sufficient terrain is shown to keep you on track. Use the maps to figure out how the various rides connect.

The elevation profiles provide a good look at what's in store by graphically showing altitude change, tread, and ratings (see page 5). Out-and-back rides are shown in only one direction. Simply reverse the direction of travel for the return profile. Note the obstacles on such rides on the way out, since their character may be different on the return. The ratings listed on the profiles are defined below.

The rest of the information is listed in an at-a-glance format. It is divided into 12 sections:

The ride number refers to where the ride falls in this guide. Use this number when cross-referencing between rides for an easy method of finding the descriptions. The ride name refers to the name of the trail. Where more than one name exists, one has been chosen that reflects the nature of the trail.

Location tells, in general, where the ride is in relation to Albuquerque.

Distance gives the ride's length in miles.

Time is an estimate of how long it will take to complete the ride. It represents trail time and does not include stops. If the ride is rated more difficult or strenuous than what you usually ride, add some time to the estimate. The scenery and physical challenge of these rides warrant plenty of stopping. As you pedal through a few of the rides in this book, compare your ride times with those listed in the guide and adjust your estimates for future rides accordingly.

Tread describes what the tires ride on when they are rubber side down.

Aerobic level estimates the physical challenge of the ride. The levels are easy, moderate, and strenuous. A note here describes what went into the rating.

Easy rides are mostly flat, but this may include some rolling hills. Any climbs will be short. Several of the easy rides include a lot of downhill.

Moderate rides will have climbs; some may be steep. Strenuous sections may occur, but the majority of the ride is moderate. Even on a moderate ride, some steeper sections may force some cyclists to dismount and walk.

Strenuous rides put the granny gear to work! The steeps may be long grueling tests of endurance, power, and determination.

Remember, these ratings are for comparison's sake. Easy rides can still have you gulping air, and moderate ones may induce you to walk. Walking a bike is a perfectly legitimate way to transport it. Also remember that this guide is for everyone, from beginners to experts. Compare your first rides to the levels listed here to get a feel for the classifications. Also bear in mind that technical sections that exceed your ability will be tiring and can make an easy or moderate ride more strenuous.

An **elevation profile** accompanies each ride description. Here the ups and downs of the route are graphed on a grid of elevation (in feet above sea level) on the left, and miles pedaled across the bottom. Route surface conditions (see map legend) and technical levels are shown on the graphs.

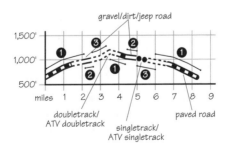

Note that these graphs are compressed (squeezed) to fit on the page. The actual slopes you will ride are not as steep as the lines drawn on the graphs (it just feels that way). Also, some extremely short dips and climbs are too small to show up on the graphs. All such abrupt changes in gradient are, however, mentioned in the mile-by-mile ride description.

Technical difficulty is not a problem with your new anti-chain-suck device. It is a scale from 1 to 5 that quantifies how much biking skill is needed to keep you in the saddle with rubber side down. Specific reasons for the rating might be listed.

Level 1: Basic bike-riding skill needed for riding smooth and obstacle-free routes. This includes graded dirt roads and sections of pavement.

Level 2: Mostly smooth tread with minor difficulties. Ruts, loose gravel, or obstacles may exist but they are easily avoided.

Level 3: Irregular tread with some rough sections, steeps, obstacles, gravel, sharp turns, and small ledge drops. This tread will have obvious route options or lines through it.

Level 4: Rough going! The tread is uneven with few smooth sections. The line is limited as it weaves through rocks (boulders, babyheads, basketballs), sand, eroded washes, downfall, and any combination of them all. These obstacles often occur on steeps!

Level 5: Continuously broken, rocky, or trenched tread with frequent, sudden, and severe changes in gradient. Slopes necessitating off-the-seat riding and a nearly continuous barrage of obstacles where the line is tough to find and unforgiving if missed.

Extreme obstacles may exist on any trail, and in this dynamic environment riders should be ready for obstacles at all times. Gauge your ability against the scale after your first few rides to get a feel for the ratings, and remember that different obstacles require different techniques.

Highlights list where to find the ride's emotional story. Qualities that make the ride unique and any special notes will be listed here.

Land status indicates the managing agency or land owner. The rides in this guide are mostly on public lands. Appendix A gives the information needed to contact the various land management agencies about rules, regulations, permits, and updates.

Maps include USGS maps that show each ride's area. These maps can be used for a more detailed view, though they may not show the ride's route. Each *Mountain Biking Albuquerque* map and profile should be sufficient for navigation and planning purposes.

Access tells you how to find the trailhead. All directions begin from the junction of Interstate 40 and Interstate 25, just north of downtown.

The ride lists where to go and how to find the way back. Attached to the descriptions are odometer readings. These are estimates! Not all bike computers are calibrated the same, but they provide a yardstick to measure against.

This guide does not pretend to be omniscient. Ratings and ride accounts are as accurate as possible. However, everyone is different. Individual riders excel in different skills and have different tastes. Use the guide as a starting point. Though regulations, ownership, and even the land itself may change, this guide will help get you home in one piece. If you have an inadvertent adventure you want to share, drop us a line.

The Journey

Albuquerque is located, more or less, in the center of the state at the interchange of Interstate 25 (north-south) and Interstate 40 (east-west). Many mountain bikers visiting Albuquerque are on a driving tour of the Southwest. If you are coming from Santa Fe, you can take Interstate 25 south, or opt for a more scenic route, the Turquoise Trail (New Mexico 14). Pick up this historic road just south of Santa Fe and drive through the "old west" towns of Golden, Madrid, and Cerrillos.

The only major route from the south is Interstate 25, up from El Paso, Texas. From Arizona, travel eastbound on Interstate 40; from Texas, travel westbound on Interstate 40.

If your journey begins by air, no problem. Albuquerque International Sunport, just southeast of town, has eight major carriers: America West, American, Continental, Delta, Frontier, Mesa, Southwest, and TWA. For general information, call 505-842-4366.

Albuquerque

Albuquerque is the largest city in New Mexico and home to one-third of the state's population, but surprisingly, finding solitude on the trail is not very hard. With over 100,000 acres of national forest adjacent to the city, Albuquerque has a playground in its own backyard.

In addition, Albuquerque Open Space, a division of Parks and Recreation, is dedicated to providing opportunities for urbanites to get out and enjoy nature. This includes mountain bikers. Open Space has started acquiring land throughout the city and designing trails with the multi-use concept in mind. They work in conjunction with the Forest Service to maintain the foothills along the western slope of the Sandias.

While on your bike, you may have much of the backcountry to yourself and forget that Albuquerque is so close. Once off your bike, this big city awaits to fulfill all of your needs. There is an active nightlife here, and you have a variety of choices, including clubs, theater, opera, and the symphony. Three cultures—Native American, Spanish, and Anglo—blend together to create New Mexico's unique and festive character, which you will find in its food, people, language, events, and architecture.

Party Time

In New Mexico, that means chiles! More chiles are grown and eaten here than anywhere in the country. Much of the cuisine is a celebration of the chile, and you will find chiles in all of the food. (I packed a green chile bagel on almost every ride.) Be sure to sample some of the state's famous dishes, such as hot tamales, stuffed sopapillas, and blue corn enchiladas. The big question is "Red or green?" (chile, that is).

Of course, you will need more than chiles after your ride, and the opportunities for good food, music, art, and entertainment are endless in Albuquerque. You could write several books on what to do and where to eat here. Contact the Albuquerque Chamber of Commerce or the Albuquerque Convention and Visitor's Bureau for information. Also, be sure to check local newspapers for listings of events. A few suggestions follow to get you started.

If you don't end up riding your bike to the crest of the Sandia Mountains (and even if you do), be sure to take the twenty-minute excursion on the Sandia Peak Tramway, the longest in North America. Enjoy a meal at the High Finance Restaurant, atop Sandia Peak, where you can often see more than 10,000 square miles. Catch the sun setting over Mount Taylor before you return to the twinkling lights of the city below.

If you happen to be in town during October, you are in luck. Every year, Albuquerque hosts the International Balloon Fiesta, the largest of its kind in the world. Spectators delight in the colorful array of balloons, which come in some very unusual designs.

On a rainy day, take a walk through Old Town Plaza, the original Spanish village settled in 1706. Visit the many museums and galleries, and check out the interesting adobe architecture.

The Rio Grande Nature Center is an inexpensive way to learn more about the area. You will find trails, exhibits, and a bookstore. This riverside forest and the nearby wetland ponds serve as a habitat for over 200 migratory and permanent-resident birds.

The Four Seasons Visitor Center is another place to go and learn more about the area, specifically the Sandia Mountains. Located on Sandia Crest at the upper tram terminal, the center sells books and brochures, provides nature and cultural tours, and includes a display of the features on the mountain.

Bike Shops

In Albuquerque, you have more bike shops than you will ever need, and most are well-equipped with everything from patches to full-suspension rigs. It is no problem to rent a bike or get a repair here.

I spent most of my time at Two Wheel Drive bicycle shop. The folks are super friendly and give great advice on where to ride. The shop keeps a chalkboard updated with current conditions of the area's most popular rides. Their website, www.twowheeldrive.com/bicycles, is also useful.

A partial list of full-service bike shops is provided in Appendix B.

Shelter

Albuquerque has a hotel/motel capacity of about 10,000! Rooms run the gamut from budget to luxurious.

Ask about bike-related rules. "Can I store my bike in my room?" is a good question to ask. Crime is a problem in Albuquerque, as in any big city, and practicing normal bike security is not always enough.

Contact New Mexico Central Reservations at 1-888-466-7829 for more information about lodging.

Amazingly enough, camping in Cibola National Forest near Albuquerque is impossible unless you want to hoist a pack and head for the backcountry. All the recreation sites function as picnic grounds, trailheads, or viewing areas.

The only developed campground in the Sandia Ranger District is Cedro Peak, which is designated a group area. It consists of two units that require advance reservations. Call 877-444-6777. The campground is set up to accommodate around 100 people and is available from May through October. This is a great location for camping while riding at Cedro Peak and Otero Canyon, but you must have a lot of friends.

In the Mountainair Ranger District, there are several developed campgrounds ranging in elevation from 6,800 to 9,600 feet. Unfortunately, you are over 45 miles from Albuquerque, but these sites may work if you plan to bike Cedro Peak and Otero Canyon, which are about 30 miles north. In general, the facilities operate from April through October on a first-come, first-served basis and only two of the campgrounds charge a fee for tent sites ($5). Tajique is your closest choice—free, open to primitive camping in the winter, and located on the Tajique-Torreon Loop.

Fortunately, several private campgrounds offer tent sites and showers around the city. There is a KOA in town and another north of town. You can get information about campgrounds from the Albuquerque Chamber of Commerce and the Albuquerque Convention and Visitor's Bureau.

Showers

There comes a time when all riders must remove the deposits of trail and perspiration accumulated upon their persons. Yes, it is possible to clean yourself in the sink of a public establishment. But it's not too cool. Think about it. Sinks are not there so bikers can prove how innovative they are at saving money. Think about the karma of the situation . . . before it breaks your chain in the middle of the desert.

Appendix C includes a list of places where you can shower for a fee. The fees range from $2 to $6. Be sure to call ahead for hours of operation. Most of the listing is YMCA or municipal pools, so plan on a swim while you're there.

Being Prepared

Mountain Biking Albuquerque is a where-to-ride book. How to ride is another story. What to bring lies in the gray area between the two subjects. Common sense is the rule here. Bring what makes you feel comfortable, but note, this is Goathead Country! I hadn't heard of these little thorns either until I moved to the Southwest. Goatheads are about the size of your pinky nail and look sort of like a goat's head. This is not good news for your tubes. You are more likely to run over a goathead below 7,200 feet and close to the city.

No matter where you ride, always use some sort of flat protection. And, if you can't replace a tube without tire levers, be sure to add them to the following equipment list.

Equipment

A necessity is a small chainring or a climbing gear. You can climb incredibly steep angles if you've got a gear low enough for your legs to spin. If the biggest rear cog (gear) is 28 or smaller, then the small chainring on the front should be 22 or smaller.

It's also important to have a way to carry lots of water. Two cages with large water bottles are the minimum. A back-borne hydration set-up is ideal.

Other equipment, like shocks, makes things nicer, but the gear ratio is most important.

Tools

Tools are a touchy subject for bikers since each has his or her own opinion. The riding here is torturous on equipment. Rock can peel the knobbies right off a tire and eat the derailleur for dessert. Keep one question in mind: "What's the farthest I'd like to walk?" I weigh out the tools and my desire not to walk, which usually results in this list:

Sense of humor
Spare tube
Patch kit
Air pump
Spare cables
Chain tool
Pocket knife
Duct tape

This list is minuscule for some and totally foreign to others. Just remember that, with time, everywhere is within walking distance.

First Aid

Consider packing a first aid kit. The most important item to put in a kit weighs nothing: prevention. Remember that safety is your responsibility. Know your biking limit and ask yourself, "How far will I be from help?" and pack accordingly. Here is a partial list to consider:

Butterfly-closure bandages
Adhesive bandages
Gauze compress pads and gauze wrap
Allergy pills
Emergency water purification tablets
Moleskin
Antiseptic swabs
Sunscreen
Energy bar
Emergency blanket

The best thing is a riding partner. Riding alone in remote areas isn't wise. If you do have a bad crash or succumb to the heat, cold, lightning, wild animals, or an act of God, remain calm and make decisions with a clear mind. Also remember the primary rule of first aid: Do no harm. This means doing only what you must to keep the injured person alive and as comfortable as possible until you can get to a doctor. For example, imagine your riding buddy goes heels over head coming down the rocky terrace of Chamisoso Canyon and is bleeding, but conscious. Stop the bleeding and get him back to town for help. With luck, you may run into help on the way out (and a pox to those who don't offer help). The point is don't waste time and don't panic. Deal with things as they come up and keep going.

Speaking of crash and burns, *always wear a helmet.* Those buff quads and powerful lungs won't go far without a brain to guide them. Some other cycling apparel also makes sense from a first-aid standpoint. Gloves will save your hands from scrapes and cuts, and cycling shorts save your butt.

Sun
The desert sun does more than just create a need for water. It can literally cook you! Sunburn is easy to combat. Use a sunscreen of at least SPF 15 and reapply it fre-

quently. Pay particular attention to your nose, cheek-bones, ears, and the nape of your neck. Sun-sensitive riders will want to take more extreme measures to blot out the sun. Some experts suggest long-sleeved, loose-fitting, white clothing. My experience has been that long sleeves are too hot and may lead to a second hazard, overheating.

Heat exhaustion is a prominent danger here, especially in summer when temperatures can reach 100 degrees F. Just being hydrated is not enough. Sometimes the body just can't keep up with rising temperatures, and its cooling system shuts down. Warning signs include pale skin, heavy sweating, nausea, weakness and dizziness, thirst, headache, and muscle cramps. If you experience any of these symptoms, find shade immediately and cool off as well as possible. Douse your head and chest with water (save some for drinking) and try to keep air moving over your skin. If you try to ride through heat exhaustion, you'll likely end up with heat stroke, a far more serious and often fatal condition.

Always wear sunglasses to protect your eyes from sun, eye strain, kamikaze insects, and flying rocks spun up by your tires. A helmet visor also helps and will keep your eyes on the trail and the sun off your nose.

The best ammo is prevention. During summer, plan to complete your ride by 9:00 A.M. or begin at 6:00 P.M. Even better, get up high. The alpine rides (near 10,000 feet) on East Mountain offer some relief. The desert is intense. Show your respect.

Water
A human's weight is 80 percent water. A desert is defined by the significant lack of water. This makes for a simple rule. Bring as much water as you can carry. Also drink lots of water before riding. Many people drink far too little water before heading out and are already dehydrated.

After you become an experienced desert rider, tailor how much fluid you bring on a ride. However, for now, bring all that can be carried. That means both water cages full with large bottles, in addition to a back-borne water bladder.

Odds are someone in your group will run out or start rationing. Share rather than ration. It's always a good idea to bring something to replenish electrolytes, too. Use the back-borne bladder for water and the bottles for electrolyte drinks.

Of course, carrying lots of water does nothing if it's just along for the ride. A body in the desert is said to need more than a gallon of water a day. Add a bit of strenuous exercise and do the math. Drink lots and drink often. Lungs dump huge amounts of moisture into exhaling breath, which, combined with sweating, quickly dehydrates the body. Don't run a quart low. Drink!

Altitude
Albuquerque straddles the Rio Grande at an elevation of about 5,000 feet, a mile above sea level. This is the magic line on the contour map where people begin to notice the altitude. Unless you live at this elevation, you may need 24 to 48 hours to feel really strong before hitting the trail.

Some of the rides in the book go as high as 10,000 feet, and while you probably won't have serious trouble with altitude sickness, you may feel tired, dizzy, or nauseous. A headache is another symptom of altitude sickness. So, slow down, get plenty of rest, drink a lot of fluids, and limit your activity for a day or so.

Weather
Did you know that this region receives an average of 300 sunny days every year? One blue-sky day after another makes Albuquerque ideal for mountain biking. Of course, there is always an exception. Surprisingly, the area has a rainy season that runs from mid-July into September. Intense thunder-

storms cause deadly lightning and wash-filling rains. When thunderheads start forming, head back to the city and visit some museums.

If caught in a storm some precautions can help keep you safe. Check how close the lightning is with the old trick of counting the seconds between the flash and the thunderclap. A count up to "five-Mississippi" means the last flash was about 1 mile distant. If the bolts are closer than a couple of miles, it's time to take cover. When in the open, ditch your bike and other metal objects. Then find a place to hunker down. Don't be the tallest thing around, and do not hide under the lone tree. The idea is to avoid being a lightning rod or hiding under one. Look for a depression or low point and crouch (don't lie down). Try to avoid puddles and moving water. It's easy to feel exposed in canyon country, but don't panic.

If you duck into a dry wash or canyon to avoid lightning, be alert for flash floods. Flash floods in the desert are beautiful events. Instant rivers shoot off of the cliffs, carving their paths just a bit deeper. But these same waters are downright ugly when you're in their path! The key is awareness. A flood can sweep through even when it's not raining in your area. Water can travel far in a desert. Listen to the radio for flash-flood warnings and heed them. If caught in a flood, don't try to outrun it. Get out of the wash to higher ground and wait.

Rain can also turn local soils into a sticky glop that is a cross between marshmallow fluff and B-movie swamp slime. It's slicker than snot and gloms on to anything it touches. The soils in the Cedro Peak and Otero Canyon area seem to be worse than elsewhere after a rain. These should be avoided during and immediately following rain. The rain does make the sand easier to ride! Right after a storm is a great time to ride the Foothills Petroglyph National Monument and along the Rio Grande.

When to Ride

You can ride the mountain biking trails around Albuquerque year-round.But conditions vary greatly throughout the area because of the different elevations of the rides—the lowest at 5,000 feet; the highest, 10,000 feet. This is good news because there is a trail out there for every season.

In general, fall is the best time to ride. The days are warm and sunny, the nights are cool, and there is little chance of wind or rain. The weather is ideal for mountain biking on all of the trails through October and the scenery is dramatic. Enjoy the colors—the yellows of aspen, the reds of maple, and the oranges of oak. The wildflowers are also spectacular during the fall.

From November to March, snow covers the higher elevations. The biking trails at Sandia Peak Ski Area close in mid-October and don't re-open until Memorial Day weekend. Good winter rides include the Foothills, the northern (lower) slopes of the Sandias, and Petroglyph National Monument. Cedro Peak and Otero Canyon are rideable during dry spells. Go early when the ground is still frozen.

Spring can be unpredictable because cold fronts are still moving through. It is usually dry and windy, but in between fronts, expect pleasant, calm conditions. The desert cactus blooms are beautiful this time of year.

Some days are just too hot in the summer to ride at the lower elevations. Head for the hills. During the early part of summer, skies are cloudless and temperatures occasionally reach 100 degrees F in the city. From late July through August, sudden thunderstorms are a real problem. Ride early, as clear mornings give way to cloudy skies and the rumbling begins.

Keep in mind that it may be 15 degrees cooler up in the Sandias, which is refreshing in the summer. Drastic changes in weather and temperature are more likely at these elevations. The mountains get about 25 inches of rainfall each year compared to about 8 inches around the city.

Riding Right!

Desert and alpine ecosystems are very fragile. Sure, it seems rugged, but the land is fragile at heart. The ways humans can damage an environment are unlimited, but keeping it safe requires only respect and knowledge. Most importantly, don't ride off the trail!

You may actually find water on the trail occasionally, but do not use it. First of all, the potholes and washes that hold rainwater are very important to the wildlife. That includes the tiny waterborne creatures that hatch, mate, and die all in the short life span of the pothole. Bikers filling water bottles kill these creatures. Secondly, sweat, skin oils, and bike by-products (such as lube) all change the chemical makeup of water. Wildlife can't fill up at a faucet when they get back to town. Don't ride through or dip into the potholes.

The nature of springs and seeps allows a bit more inter-action. They are often rock-filtered and quite fresh. However, unless you know that a particular spring is safe, don't drink from it. Canoncito Spring near the Faulty Trail is a popular watering hole, but it is unregulated. Another such spring is at mile 2 of the 10K-Ellis Loop.

If you find yourself in a situation where you need to use the available water, be forewarned. Most portable water filters do not remove toxic materials. If you must drink the water, limit your intake to the amount needed to get you back to civilization. Use a filter to remove bacteria and other gut-loving life. Springs are the best.

IMBA Rules of the Trail

Here are some guidelines for riding right, reprinted by permission from the International Mountain Bicycling Association (IMBA), whose mission is to promote environmentally sound and socially responsible mountain biking. The basic theme here is to reduce or eliminate any damage to land and water, plant and wildlife inhabitants, and other backcountry visitors and trail users. Ride with respect.

Thousands of miles of dirt trails have been closed to mountain bicyclists. The irresponsible riding habits of a few riders have been a factor. Do your part to maintain trail access by observing the following rules of the trail:

1. Ride on open trails only. Respect trail and road closures (ask if not sure), avoid possible trespass on private land, obtain permits and authorization as may be required. Federal and state wilderness areas are closed to cycling. The way you ride will influence trail management decisions and policies.

2. Leave no trace. Be sensitive to the dirt beneath you. Even on open (legal) trails, you should not ride under conditions where you will leave evidence of your passing, such as on certain soils after a rain. Recognize different types of soil and trail construction; practice low-impact cycling. This also means staying on existing trails and not creating any new ones. Be sure to pack out at least as much as you pack in.

3. Control your bicycle! Inattention for even a second can cause problems. Obey all bicycle speed regulations and recommendations.

4. Always yield trail. Make known your approach well in advance. A friendly greeting (or bell) is considerate and works well; don't startle others. Show your respect when passing by, slowing to a walking pace or even stopping. Anticipate other trail users around corners or in blind spots.

5. Never spook animals. All animals are startled by an unannounced approach, a sudden movement, or a loud noise. This can be dangerous for you, others, and the animals. Give animals extra room and time to adjust to you. When passing horses use special care and follow directions from the horseback riders (ask if uncertain). Running cattle and disturbing wildlife are serious offenses. Leave gates as you found them, or as marked.

6. Plan ahead. Know your equipment, your ability, and the area in which you are riding and prepare accordingly. Be self-sufficient at all times, keep your equipment in good repair, and carry necessary supplies for changes in weather or other conditions. A well-executed trip is a satisfaction to you and not a burden or offense to others. Always wear a helmet.

Keep trails open by setting a good example of environmentally sound and socially responsible off-road cycling.

Albuquerque now has a club affiliated with IMBA called Trail Partners. They hope to expand the riding opportunities in the area and maintain the existing trails. Trail Partners follows trail issues and organizes group rides. For more information, contact Mark Reineke or Margie Tatro, 75 Canyon Road, Sandia Park, New Mexico 87047.

Otero Canyon

Otero Canyon West

Location: In the Otero Canyon area near the town of Tijeras; about 20 miles east of Albuquerque.

Distance: 7.7-mile loop.

Time: 1 to 2 hours.

Tread: 7.7 miles on singletrack.

Aerobic level: Strenuous. About 1 mile of serious climbing, then a good mix of gradual climbs and level riding. The 3-mile descent is a blast.

Technical difficulty: 3 to 4. Occasional tight turns and technical rocky sections, plus a hard 0.3-mile climb on loose rock and staircases that rate a 4.

Highlights: Otero Canyon offers excellent hard-packed singletrack in a beautiful limestone canyon. This multi-use trail system is the result of a joint effort by the biking and equestrian communities. Hopefully work will continue in the area.

The 3 miles of fast and technical downhill are the best around. This is pinyon-juniper country that also has a neat little wetland community of cottonwood trees and cattails in the canyon.

Two Wheel Drive bicycle shop puts out a large detailed map of the area that is a must for any rider who spends time here. The map covers Otero Canyon, as well as Cedro Peak Area and the rides near Oak Flat Picnic Area.

Land status: Cibola National Forest.

Maps: The Trails of Cedro Peak and Otero Canyon, available at Two Wheel Drive bicycle shop and the Sandia Ranger Station, and USGS Tijeras.

Access: Travel east from Albuquerque on Interstate 40 for about 15 miles to Exit 175 at Tijeras. Veer right off the interstate and go straight through the four-way stop onto New Mexico 337. Pass the office of the Tijeras Ranger District after 0.5 mile. You can pick up area information here and visit the ruins of the Tijeras Pueblo, a 700-year-old Anasazi village. Then, continue another 3.2 miles and park in a small gravel area on the right. A sign indicates Trail 56.

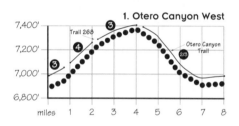

1. Otero Canyon West

The Ride

0.0   Head down the old paved road and take the first trail to the left. You will cross a small creek.

0.4   Trail junction. Just before crossing Otero Canyon, take the trail up and to the right instead. A trail marker indicates that this is Tunero Trail. *Tunero* is the Spanish word for tunnel. Be ready for a few fun moves and one hard but short staircase on your climb.

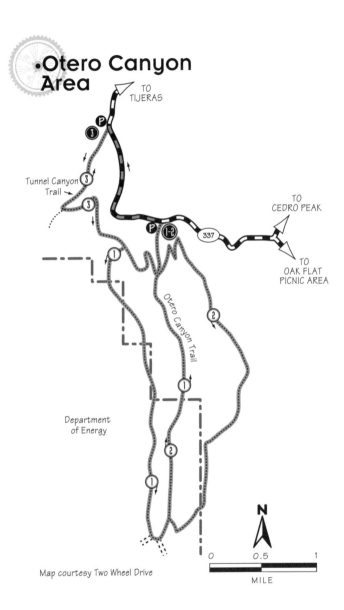

•Otero Canyon Area

TO TIJERAS

P 3

Tunnel Canyon Trail → 3

3

P 1-2

337

TO CEDRO PEAK

TO OAK FLAT PICNIC AREA

1

Otero Canyon Trail

2

1

Department of Energy

2

1

N

Map courtesy Two Wheel Drive

0   0.5   1

MILE

1.0 At the three-way trail junction, turn left. This is Trail 268 on the map put out by Two Wheel Drive bicycle shop. Locals refer to this trail as "Rambo" because you may occasionally see a uniformed military officer. Begin with a nasty climb. You may find the loose rock impossible to negotiate.

1.3 Gain ridgetop and enjoy occasional views. The next couple miles include mostly level riding with some up and down. The rocky sections are short and rideable. Pass signs on your right indicating no trespassing.

3.6 Reach a three-way trail junction and go left.

4.3 Ignore the trail to the right and head down a steep, rocky portion of trail.

4.4 Somewhat confusing trail junction. Take the nice singletrack to the left. If you are on course, you will soon pass a trail off to the right and begin accelerating down, down, downhill. Enjoy and ride fast. There are only a couple technical spots, and of course, some rocks.

7.1 Otero Canyon opens up. Fly over smooth rollercoaster hills.

7.3 Return to the initial trail junction. Go left over the canyon and right back to the trailhead.

7.7 End of ride.

Otero Canyon East

See map on page 24

Location: In the Otero Canyon area near the town of Tijeras; about 20 miles east of Albuquerque.

Distance: 7.9-mile loop.

Time: 1 to 2 hours.

Tread: 7.9 miles on singletrack.

Aerobic level: Strenuous. A great mix of stiff climbing, some level riding, and an awesome downhill.

Technical difficulty: 3 to 4. The obstacles are not too bad. Have fun with the rideable staircases, skinny trail, and technical rocky sections. The loose rock on a few of the climbs is cruel and rates a 5.

Highlights: Just like Otero Canyon West, the loop on the east side of Otero offers excellent singletrack and an awesome downhill through the limestone canyon. You will take Blue Ribbon Trail along the east ridge and come back down through Otero Canyon. You could ride this loop counterclockwise to change your direction in the canyon, but why miss the best 2 miles of downhill around. The switchbacks that take you almost to the top of the east ridge are great. Then, as with most of the rides in the area, you must endure some serious climbing on loose rock and staircases. With that behind you, Otero Canyon East serves up a little smoother singletrack and more variety than the trail to the west.

Land status: Cibola National Forest.

Maps: The Trails of Cedro Peak and Otero Canyon, available at Two Wheel Drive bicycle shop and the Sandia Ranger Station, and USGS Tijeras.

Access: Travel east from Albuquerque on Interstate 40 for about 15 miles to Exit 175 at Tijeras. Veer right off the interstate and go straight through the four-way stop onto New Mexico 337. Pass the office of the Tijeras Ranger District after 0.5 mile. Then, continue another 3.2 miles and park in a small gravel area on the right. A sign indicates Trail 56.

The Ride

0.0 Head down the old paved road and take the first trail to the left. You will cross a small creek.

0.4 Trail junction. Turn left at the first trail sign and cross Otero Canyon. Then hang an immediate left onto Trail 236, or Blue Ribbon Trail.

0.6 The first switchback in the climb to the ridge includes a difficult staircase.

1.2 After the third switchback, begin the final push to the ridgetop on terribly loose rock. Even the best riders will spin out or have to put a foot down.

1.5 Gain the ridgetop. When the trail forks, you can go either way. (Ignore the painted markers on the trees.)

1.7 Trail forks. Stay left with the main trail. After some loose rock, enter an open meadow and travel straight across.

2.1 Cross a doubletrack. A mile of smooth, hard-packed trail lies ahead. Good fun followed by a class 4 rocky climb.

3.1 An old roadbed joins from the right. Continue straight.

3.3 Go straight through the four-way intersection.

4.0 At the T intersection, take the doubletrack right, which narrows quickly to singletrack.

4.5 Take a right at the three-way intersection. Soon after, an inviting trail joins from the left. Continue straight.

4.6 At the fork, bear right downhill. After a steep, rocky descent, you will be riding down Otero Canyon.

7.3 Otero Canyon opens up. Fly over smooth rollercoaster hills.

7.5 Return to the initial trail junction. Go left over the canyon and right back to the trailhead.

7.9 End of ride.

Tunnel Canyon Loop

See map on page 24

Location: In the Otero Canyon area near the town of Tijeras; about 20 miles east of Albuquerque.

Distance: 4.2-mile loop.

Time: 30 to 45 minutes.

Tread: 3 miles on singletrack and 1.2 miles on pavement.

Aerobic level: Moderate. A gentle climb is followed by a more difficult grunt to the ridge above Otero Canyon. Then, it's all downhill.

Technical difficulty: 3. Encounter tight turns and technical sections of loose rock. A couple of relatively easy staircases add a fun challenge.

Highlights: Tunnel Canyon is just as beautiful as Otero, and may be greener and even more pleasant. The singletrack up this tight canyon climbs gently and includes lots of fun sidehills.

You will climb more steeply as you head up and out of Tunnel Canyon, then enjoy some skinny trail and exposure. Slow down to take in the view of the Sandias before zooming down a short technical section into Otero Canyon. The obstacles are nothing but fun on this ride.

This ride will be too short for most mountain bikers. Combine it with either of the first two rides in the book for a super approach into Otero Canyon.

Land status: Cibola National Forest.

Maps: The Trails of Cedro Peak and Otero Canyon, available at Two Wheel Drive bicycle shop and the Sandia Ranger Station, and USGS Tijeras.

Access: Travel east from Albuquerque on Interstate 40 for about 15 miles to Exit 175 at Tijeras. Veer right off the interstate and go straight through the four-way stop onto New Mexico 337. Pass the office of the Tijeras Ranger District after 0.5 mile. Then, continue another 2 miles and park in a small gravel area on the right. A sign indicates Trail 14.

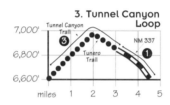

The Ride

0.0 Ride out of the parking lot and down the singletrack. The trail is marked here with a brown Forest Service sign as 14. Enjoy gradual climbing through Tunnel Canyon.

0.9 Important! Sharp hairpin; go left. The trail ahead leads to nowhere, believe me! Continue climbing more steeply and level out with big views of the Sandias. Cedro Peak is the mountain to the right with the towers. Some of this stretch is narrow and rather exposed.

2.0 Trail junction. Go straight and ride downhill. You'll encounter a couple hard moves and one tricky staircase.

2.6 Reach Otero Canyon; go left down the dry streambed.

2.9 Cross a small creek and ride a short steep up to an old paved road. Turn right.

3.0 Reach NM 337 and turn left onto pavement.

4.2 Turn left into the parking area at the trailhead.

Cedro Peak Area

Coyote and Chamisoso Trails

Location: In the Cedro Peak area near the town of Tijeras; about 20 miles east of Albuquerque.

Distance: 9.9-mile loop.

Time: 1.5 to 2.5 hours.

Tread: 9.1 miles on singletrack and 0.8 mile on dirt road.

Aerobic level: Strenuous. A couple of grueling hills on loose rock.

Technical difficulty: 4 to 5. Much of the trail is fun class 3 singletrack, so do not be scared away by the rating. Some of the climbs on the Coyote Trail are loose rock and technical staircases. Many riders will have to walk some of the first half a mile of the Chamisoso Trail.

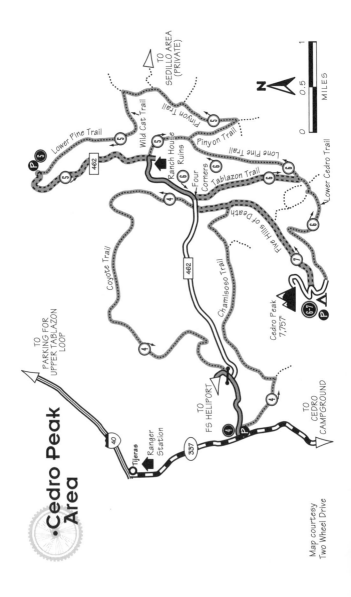

Cedro Peak Area

TO SEDILLO AREA (PRIVATE)

Lower Pine Trail

Wild Cat Trail

Pinyon Trail

Pinyon Trail

462

Ranch House Ruins

Lone Pine Trail

Four Corners

Tablazon Trail

Lower Cedro Trail

Coyote Trail

Five Hills of Death

462

Chamisoso Trail

Cedro Peak
7,757'

TO PARKING FOR UPPER TABLAZON LOOP

40

Tijeras

Ranger Station

337

F5 HELIPORT

TO CEDRO CAMPGROUND

N

MILES
0   0.5   1

Map courtesy
Two Wheel Drive

Highlights: Coyote Trail is super fun with several challenging climbs, and many mountain bikers consider Chamisoso the prettiest canyon around Albuquerque. This adds up to make one of the best loops in the book. The variety of terrain on this ride is a big plus. Coyote Trail mixes smooth, hard-packed singletrack with difficult rocky climbs. Then, after the initial white-knuckle descent on Chamisoso Trail, you can zoom down the rest of the canyon with little worry. Have a blast and come back to ride this loop in the opposite direction.

Land status: Cibola National Forest.

Maps: The Trails of Cedro Peak and Otero Canyon, available at Two Wheel Drive bicycle shop and the Sandia Ranger Station, and USGS Sedillo.

Access: Travel east from Albuquerque on Interstate 40 for about 15 miles to Exit 175 at Tijeras. Veer right off the interstate and go straight through the four-way stop onto New Mexico 337. Pass the office of the Tijeras Ranger District after 0.5 mile. Then, continue another 0.8 mile and turn left onto Forest Road 462. Park immediately on the right in a dirt lot.

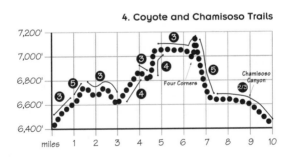

4. Coyote and Chamisoso Trails

The Ride

0.0   Leave the parking area and head up FR 462. The ride begins with a gradual climb. Soon, pass a trail on the right, where you will finish the loop.

0.6   FR 462 forks right. Continue straight.

0.7   Before the gate, which leads to the Forest Service Heliport, pick up the singletrack on the right and enjoy level riding.

1.3   Begin to climb, then stay left. An old jeep road continues straight ahead.

1.4   Ride fast downhill on smooth singletrack alongside a small canyon. Finish the 0.3-mile descent with a scary move on a narrow wooden bridge.

2.0   Encounter the first difficult section on broken trail, loose rock, and staircases.

2.2   The trail splits here. Go either way up a bad staircase. Most riders will be walking this.

2.5   Enter a grassy meadow and enjoy a smooth 0.5-mile descent.

2.9   The trail forks. Go left and work hard for a mile ascending over loose rock.

4.1   Catch your breath and take in the panoramic view of the Sandias.

4.6   At the fork, go right and climb some more rocky terrain.

5.5   Begin a much needed descent.

6.1   Reach Four Corners, a major crossroads in the Cedro Peak area. Go straight across FR 462 and up a wide gravel road (Trail 13).

6.2   Stay right everywhere as you ascend Trail 13 and look for a singletrack trail on the right. This is the white-knuckle, class 5 descent. Quite a wild ride.

6.9 A side trail enters from the left. The technical aspect of the descent eases a bit as you enter the prettiest canyon around. Slow down and enjoy. This tiny singletrack is fast and relatively smooth.

8.4 A short side trail right leads up to FR 462. Continue straight down the canyon.

8.9 Go under a set of powerlines. A side trail enters from the left. Make a hard right turn here.

9.8 Reach FR 462 and turn left.

9.9 Return to the parking area off NM 337.

Pinyon, Wild Cat, and Lower Pine Trails

See map on page 32

Location: In the Cedro Peak area near the town of Tijeras; about 20 miles east of Albuquerque.

Distance: 7.6-mile loop.

Time: 1 to 2 hours.

Tread: 5.6 miles on singletrack and 2 miles on dirt road.

Aerobic level: Moderate. There are several long but gradual climbs.

Technical difficulty: 3 to 4. Some class 2 riding on this loop, but Wild Cat can shake a few screws loose and Lower Pine serves up good technical moves.

Highlights: This is another great ride in the Cedro Peak area with plenty of options for creating longer loops. Pinyon Trail consists of hard-packed singletrack with only a modest grade. Quite a pleasure. Wild Cat Trail is a wild ride—downhill and extremely rocky. It's hard not to put a foot down here and there. And finally, Lower Pine Trail. This excellent, technical singletrack deserves the four stars it gets on the trail map put out by Two Wheel Drive bicycle shop.

Land status: Cibola National Forest.

Maps: The Trails of Cedro Peak and Otero Canyon, available at Two Wheel Drive bicycle shop and the Sandia Ranger Station, and USGS Sedillo.

Access: Travel east from Albuquerque on Interstate 40 for about 15 miles to Exit 175 at Tijeras. Veer right off the interstate and turn left at the four-way stop onto New Mexico 333. Travel 3.3 miles and turn right onto Baca Bartels Road. Immediately reach a fork and go right onto Kennedy Road. After 0.7 mile, come to a T intersection and turn right onto Forest Road. Follow this road for 0.3 mile and turn right onto Forest Road 462. The trailhead parking is 0.1 mile on the left. A sign indicates Trail 11D.

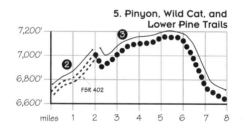

The Ride

0.0 Ride up FR 462, which starts off with a gradual climb. Trail 11D is your return route.

0.6 The trail levels off and opens up to a good view of Cedro Peak straight ahead. At the fork, go left.

1.0 At the next fork, go left again.

1.2 Pass a dirt road on the right. Continue straight. Respect the private property off to the right.

1.5 Crest out at the top of a long hill. Another dirt road enters on the right. Continue straight.

2.0 Reach a crossroads at Ranch House Ruins and turn left.

2.2 Rocky terrain leads downhill through an old metal gate. Pass the southern end of Lower Pine Trail. The trail is not marked here. Continue straight.

2.8 Reach a three-way intersection with big views of the Sandias. Bear left. The trail to the right is Lone Pine.

3.8 Reach a four-way junction in a saddle, take a sharp left, and continue on Pinyon.

4.4 Pass a side trail, Squirrel Run, on the right.

5.1 At the Y intersection in a small field keep left.

5.5 Turn left onto Wild Cat Trail. A faded sign marks the trailhead. Loosen up and be ready for some hard, rocky moves.

6.4 With that wild ride behind you, turn right onto Lower Pine Trail at the T intersection. This is a fun mile, mostly downhill, with solid class 3 terrain.

7.6 Reach the parking area.

Lower Cedro, Lone Pine, and Tablazon Trails

See map on page 32

Location: In the Cedro Peak area near the town of Tijeras; about 20 miles east of Albuquerque.

Distance: 9.6-mile loop.

Time: 2 to 3 hours.

Tread: 6.7 miles on singletrack, 2.5 miles on doubletrack, and 0.4 mile on dirt road.

Aerobic level: Moderate. The climbs are short and gradual and the level riding is certainly a pleasure.

Technical difficulty: 4. You can't hide from the loose rock and staircases that are characteristic of the area, but much of this loop is hard-packed and smooth. If you walk, it is just for a short distance.

Highlights: In the Cedro Peak Area, you will find some of Albuquerque's finest mountain biking. Lone Pine Trail is considered one of the best singletrack trails around. Don't miss this ride. These foothills are covered with juniper, pinyon, and oak. In addition to awesome singletrack, the highlights include beautiful Tablazon Canyon and an occasional view of the Sandias. Follow the ride description closely. You will encounter a large network of trails here.

Note: The small mountain above the parking area is Cedro Peak, elevation 7,757 feet.

Land status: Cibola National Forest.

Maps: The Trails of Cedro Peak and Otero Canyon, available at Two Wheel Drive bicycle shop and the Sandia Ranger Station, and USGS Sedillo.

Access: Travel east from Albuquerque on Interstate 40 for about 15 miles to Exit 175 at Tijeras. Veer right off the interstate and go straight through the four-way stop onto New Mexico 337. Pass the office of the Tijeras Ranger District after 0.5 mile. Then, continue another 4.2 miles and turn left onto Juan Tomas Road (Forest Road 242). The road is marked with a sign for Cedro Peak Campground. After 0.6 mile, turn left onto Forest Road 252, which is also well marked. Travel 1.5 miles to Cedro Peak Campground (for groups by reservation only), and then another 0.2 mile to the trailhead parking lot on the left.

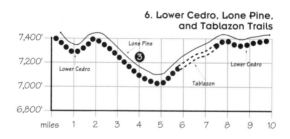

6. Lower Cedro, Lone Pine,
and Tablazon Trails

The Ride

0.0	Ride out of the parking lot to the right and down FR 252 to the campground.
0.2	Turn left onto Trail 252B (Lower Cedro Trail), the lower of the two trails across from the campground.
2.2	Reach the junction with Trail 252C and turn right.
2.3	At this T intersection, turn left.

2.4 The Y intersection of Trail 12 (Tablazon Trail) and Trail 11 (Lone Pine Trail). Take the right fork up Lone Pine Trail, which is often listed as the best singletrack in the area. After a steep, rocky ascent, the trail levels out into beautiful, smooth singletrack.

3.5 Follow the trail left down what looks like a rocky run-off. The narrow singletrack in the woods to the right leads into the Sedillo area, which is mostly private land.

4.1 At the T intersection, turn left. This area can be confusing. There is a large open field where puzzled mountain bikers have created short, dead-end trails. Enjoy good views of the Sandias to the north.

4.7 An unmarked trail (Lower Pine Trail) intersects on the right. Continue straight up a rocky hill and through an old gate.

4.9 Four-way trail junction. Ruins from a stone house to the left. FR 462 north to the right. Continue straight on the rocky doubletrack, which is now FR 462 south.

5.7 Turn left onto Trail 12 (Tablazon Trail) and enjoy this 1.5-mile stretch of doubletrack through a meadow. This leg of the ride might be closed in the future. (Consider the alternate "Five Hills of Death," which is 0.1 mile farther and marked on the map as Trail 13. You will reach FR 252 just north of the trailhead parking after 2.5 miles if you make it up this rocky staircase.)

7.2 Return to the Y intersection of Trails 12 and 11. Continue straight to retrace the initial 2.4 miles of the ride.

7.3 Be sure to turn right onto 252C.

7.4 Be sure to turn left onto Trail 252B (Lower Cedro Trail).

9.4 Reach the campground and turn right on the dirt road.

9.6 Return to your vehicle at the trailhead parking lot.

Five Hills of Death

See map on page 32

Location: In the Cedro Peak area near the town of Tijeras; about 20 miles east of Albuquerque.

Distance: 2.5 miles one way.

Time: 20 minutes to 1 hour.

Tread: 2.5 miles on doubletrack, which feels like singletrack because there is usually only one line through the loose rock.

Aerobic level: Easy. You are going downhill. But if you add this trail to another ride and decide to climb—strenuous!

Technical difficulty: 5. For many riders, sections of this trail become a bike-hike. Several of the descents are continuous broken and rocky tread. Where is the line?

Highlights: The trail may have gotten its name from the aerobic difficulty when climbing, but the title refers adequately to the technical challenges whether you are going up or down. The staircases and loose rock are the worst. Five Hills has actually been part of a racecourse for several local events in the past. This stretch of trail is a good example of how the terrain in the area can change each year from rain and traffic. Sometimes it is rideable, and sometimes it is not. You can access every trail in the Cedro Peak area from Five Hills (see the map). Give it a try, downhill first, and decide whether to add it to another loop.

Land status: Cibola National Forest.

Maps: The Trails of Cedro Peak and Otero Canyon, available at Two Wheel Drive bicycle shop and the Sandia Ranger Station, and USGS Sedillo.

Access: Travel east from Albuquerque on Interstate 40 for about 15 miles to Exit 175 at Tijeras. Veer right off the interstate and go straight through the four-way stop onto New Mexico 337. Pass the office of the Tijeras Ranger District after 0.5 mile. Then, continue another 4.2 miles and turn left onto Juan Tomas Road (Forest Road 242). The road is marked with a sign for Cedro Peak Campground. After 0.6 mile, turn left onto Forest Road 252, which is also well marked. Travel 1.5 miles to Cedro Peak Campground (for groups by reservation only), and then another 0.2 mile to the trailhead parking lot on the left.

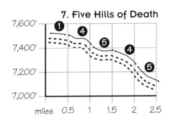

The Ride

- **0.0** Ride out of the parking lot to the left up FR 252 toward Cedro Peak.
- **0.1** At the T intersection, turn right onto Forest Road 240, which leads to the top of the peak.
- **0.2** Turn right onto doubletrack, unmarked Trail 13, or Five Hills of Death. Good luck!
- **2.5** Reach FR 462 at Four Corners. Lots of options here.

Oak Flat Area

Gambles Oak and Mahogany Trails

Location: In the Oak Flat area south of the town of Tijeras; about 25 miles east of Albuquerque.

Distance: 7.4-mile loop.

Time: 1 to 2 hours.

Tread: 6.8 miles on singletrack and 0.6 mile on doubletrack or old dirt road.

Aerobic level: Moderate. Gentle up and down with a lot of level riding.

Technical difficulty: 3. A great place for beginners to try some challenging singletrack without walking most of the ride. The obstacles are minimal and include tight turns, narrow trail, and short sections of loose rock.

Highlights: This ride is one of the easiest on the Two Wheel Drive bicycle shop map "The Trails of Cedro Peak and Otero Canyon." A good place to start if you are not sure of your technical skills on loose rock and staircases. While the scenery is not too impressive, the trail conditions are good. Intermediate riders may be able to ride the loop clean, and quite fast. A lot of level riding with just enough challenges to keep it interesting. For

•Oak Flat Area

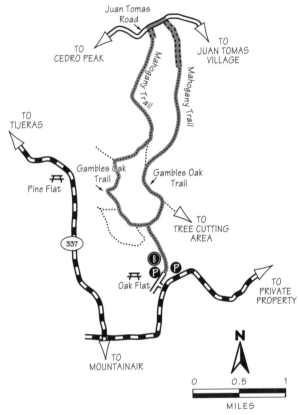

Juan Tomas Road

TO
CEDRO PEAK

TO
JUAN TOMAS
VILLAGE

Mahogany Trail

Mahogany Trail

TO
TIJERAS

Pine Flat

337

Gambles Oak
Trail

Gambles Oak
Trail

TO
TREE CUTTING
AREA

Oak Flat

TO
PRIVATE
PROPERTY

TO
MOUNTAINAIR

N

0   0.5   1

MILES

Map courtesy Two Wheel Drive

more riding in the area, consult the map mentioned above. Be aware: Some of the trails just east of this loop have been affected by a tree removal project. Route-finding is interesting to say the least.

Land status: Cibola National Forest.

Maps: The Trails of Cedro Peak and Otero Canyon, available at Two Wheel Drive bicycle shop and the Sandia Ranger Station, and USGS Sedillo.

Access: Travel east from Albuquerque on Interstate 40 for about 15 miles to Exit 175 at Tijeras. Veer right off the interstate and go straight through the four-way stop onto New Mexico 337. Pass the office of the Tijeras Ranger District after 0.5 mile. Then, after about 7 miles, turn left onto Oak Flat Road where a sign marks the Forest Service picnic area. Follow this road for about 1 mile to the picnic area on the left. Signs direct you to Oak Flat Picnic Area; take a right at the T intersection and a right at the fork. Park in one of the first few spaces on the right as you enter the lot. (This parking lot is closed each year from October 31 to May 1. For an alternate parking spot, travel 0.1 mile past the picnic area to a pull-off on the right. Ride back into the picnic area to the trailhead, about 0.3 mile total.)

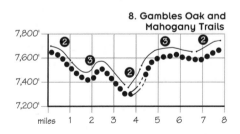

45

The Ride

0.0 Head into the woods just before the first white lines on the pavement to the right and go left on the singletrack.

0.1 Turn right onto an old dirt road, then pick up singletrack again on the left within about 0.1 mile.

0.4 Cross an old dirt road, then another at mile 0.7.

0.8 Reach Gambles Oak Trail and turn left. Enjoy some fun rocky moves as you descend.

1.1 Ignore the trail on your left, which leads to Pine Flat Picnic Area. Continue straight.

1.3 At the fork, stay right. The left fork also leads to Pine Flat Picnic Area.

1.9 Begin riding on the Mahogany Trail. Another side trail leads left. Continue straight and climb ever so slightly.

2.3 The trail to the right is a cut-off (see map). Stay left and ride fast downhill on the smooth singletrack.

3.2 Enter a large meadow and travel alongside a dry canyon on very narrow trail.

3.7 Cross an old dirt road and follow the singletrack straight ahead.

3.9 Reach the gravel Juan Tomas Road. Turn right.

4.0 Look carefully to pick up an unmarked doubletrack trail on the right. You will encounter fairly level riding for a while.

4.6 As the trail narrows to singletrack, begin climbing and tackle some technical, rocky moves.

5.6 The trail to the right is the east side of the cut-off trail. Continue straight.

6.3 Be sure to turn right here. A sign indicates Gambles Oak Trail.

6.6 Turn left on the entrance trail where you began the loop and retrace your path to the parking area.

7.4 End of ride.

Manzano Mountains

Tajique-Torreon Loop

Location: The eastern slope of the Manzano Mountains through the towns of Tajique and Torreon; about 50 miles southeast of Albuquerque.

Distance: 20-mile loop.

Tread: 17.5 miles on dirt road and 2.5 miles on pavement.

Time: 2 to 3 hours.

Aerobic level: Moderate. The elevation gain during the first half of the ride is gentle—a piece of cake on this graded dirt road.

Technical difficulty: 1. No obstacles, just leaf-looker traffic.

Highlights: Save this ride for a gorgeous autumn day when you want to get out for a spin and enjoy the countryside. This area is known for its impressive stands of Bigtooth maples, which blaze deep red every fall—the highlight of the foliage display. As you ride up Tajique Canyon, enjoy views of the Manzanos to the west. For much of the ride you will travel through a dense forest of oak, aspen, and ponderosa pine. Fall colors appear about the same time as the Albuquerque Balloon Fiesta—the first two weeks in October. Tajique and Torreon are small Spanish villages with several historic

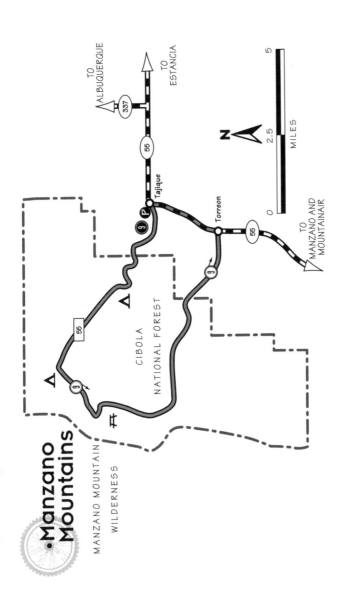

Manzano Mountains

MANZANO MOUNTAIN WILDERNESS

CIBOLA NATIONAL FOREST

TO ALBUQUERQUE

TO ESTANCIA

337

55

Tajique

Torreon

TO MANZANO AND MOUNTAINAIR

N

0   2.5   5

MILES

churches and a few artisans. A visit during the apple harvest is a plus!

Note: The area around Fourth of July Campground is extremely popular in October. Traffic on weekends is heavy and travel along Forest Road 55 can be dangerous.

Land status: Cibola National Forest. You will cross private property several times at the beginning and end of the loop.

Maps: USGS Bosque Peak, Capilla Peak, Tajique, and Torreon; and the pocket guide to the Sandia and Mountainair Districts of Cibola National Forest.

Access: Travel east from Albuquerque on Interstate 40 for 15 miles to Exit 175 at Tijeras. Veer right off the interstate and go straight through the four-way stop onto New Mexico 337. Pass the office of the Sandia Ranger District after 0.5 mile. Then, continue south for another 27 miles to a T intersection. Turn right onto New Mexico 55, travel 3 miles to the town of Tajique, and ask permission to park across from Ray's Store.

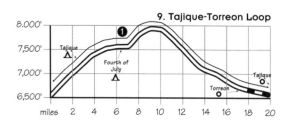

The Ride

- **0.0** Just past Ray's Store, turn right onto Forest Road 55 and head toward Fourth of July Campground.
- **3.0** Pass Tajique Campground on the left.
- **3.5** Pass Forest Road 322 on the left.

4.6 Pass Forest Road 321 on the right.

5.3 FR 55A forks left and leads to a Baptist youth camp; continue straight.

6.4 Access to Albuquerque Trail 78 on the right.

6.9 Reach Fourth of July Campground. For the next 7 miles the road is marked as primitive and traffic is uncommon.

8.2 Access to Cedro Blanco Trail 79 on the right.

9.1 Picnic area on the right and access to Bosque Trail 174.

11.3 Access to Trail Canyon 170 on the right.

13.1 Leave the national forest.

14.0 A road joins from the right; continue straight.

17.5 Reach NM 55 in Torreon and turn left onto pavement.

20.0 Return to Ray's Store and have a soda.

East Mountain

Faulty Trail

Location: The eastern slope of the Sandias off the Crest Highway; about 30 miles northeast of Albuquerque.

Distance: 12.8-mile loop.

Time: 3 to 4 hours.

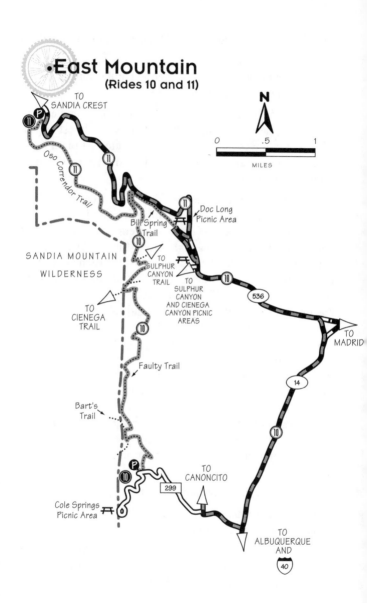

•East Mountain
(Rides 10 and 11)

N

TO
SANDIA CREST

Oso Corredor Trail

0   .5   1
MILES

Doc Long
Picnic Area

Bill Spring
Trail

SANDIA MOUNTAIN

WILDERNESS

TO
SULPHUR
CANYON
TRAIL

TO
SULPHUR
CANYON
AND CIENEGA
CANYON PICNIC
AREAS

536

TO
CIENEGA
TRAIL

Faulty Trail

Bart's
Trail

TO
MADRID

14

P

10

TO
CANONCITO

299

Cole Springs
Picnic Area

TO
ALBUQUERQUE
AND
40

Tread: 6 miles on singletrack, 1.2 miles on dirt road, and 5.6 miles on pavement.

Aerobic level: Strenuous. Some good climbs, but the paved stretch is almost all downhill.

Technical difficulty: 4 to 5. Basically you have singletrack-rated solid class 3 interrupted by sections with almost impossible rocky moves. Several short climbs are just plain loose rock. Unless you are an extremely talented rider, expect to be hiking some of this ride.

Highlights: This ride offers incredible views, crosses several intermittent streams, and travels through beautiful alpine forest, but you must be up for the challenge. The sections of good singletrack come at a high price. Much of the trail is expert only (or walk it!). Faulty Trail must be reached by other trails, which is part of the adventure. Canoncito Trail goes straight up a ridge following a stream to its source before reaching Faulty Trail, but you may find the travertine pools are worth the time off the bike. Faulty Trail traverses East Mountain about midway up along a geological fault line, hence the trail's official name. No one is sure who cleared this trail in 1975, so it was once called Mystery Trail. The mysterious ones slashed diamond shapes on the trees to mark it, so some bikers still call it Diamond Trail.

Note: While this loop takes you out Bill Spring Trail to Doc Long Picnic Area, an extension, Oso Corredor Trail, at mile 4.8, connects you to 10K–Tree Spring Loop and trails at the Sandia Peak Ski Area.

Land status: Cibola National Forest.

Maps: USGS Sandia Crest, Sandia Peak, Tijeras; and the national forest map of Sandia Ranger District.

Access: Travel east from Albuquerque on Interstate 40 for about 15 miles to Exit 175. Follow New Mexico 14 north toward Cedar Crest for 3.5 miles and turn left onto Forest Road

299. A sign indicates Cole Springs Picnic Area. After 0.5 mile, the road forks. Take the left fork, which is a dirt road, and continue toward the picnic area. You will cross the national forest boundary after 1.1 miles and the trailhead parking is another 0.1 mile on the right.

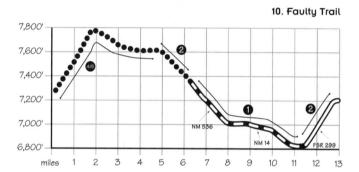

10. Faulty Trail

The Ride

0.0 Start on the singletrack to the right marked Canoncito Trail, not Barts Trail.

0.6 Reach the travertine pools and climb (walk) up and along the creek for 0.1 mile.

0.7 At the top, in an open area suitable for camping, follow the trail on either side of the creek to Canoncito Spring and a junction marked with a wooden sign. Be sure to take Faulty Trail right. Bikes are not allowed in the wilderness area.

1.3 A side trail on the right. Continue straight and enjoy a 0.5-mile stretch of awesome singletrack.

1.8 Cross a creek and climb (walk!) up the other side of the ridge. Each time you cross a streambed, expect to walk up a steep rocky section.

3.0 Reach a rocky outcrop with superb views, then descend steeply on a very narrow section of trail.

3.2 Cross Cienega Trail. This steep, rocky ascent includes some stone stairs.

3.4 A horse trail enters from the right in a sharp turn, then enjoy smooth downhill on switchbacks.

3.5 Cross Sulphur Trail. Another steep, rocky ascent followed by a technical downhill stretch.

4.8 Oso Corredor Trail spurs off left; continue straight.

5.1 Faulty Trail becomes Bill Spring Trail. This great downhill stretch is wide in places and follows a stream below the spring through stands of large oak trees.

6.0 Reach a paved path adjacent to Doc Long Picnic Area and continue straight.

6.9 Get off your bike to cross a ditch right before New Mexico 536. Turn right and fly downhill on the paved Crest Highway.

8.7 At the intersection with four-lane NM 14, turn right. Ride downhill at first, then get ready for a big climb.

11.1 Turn right onto FR 299.

11.6 Fork left onto the gravel road heading for Cole Springs Picnic Area.

12.7 Cross a boundary into Cibola National Forest.

12.8 Return to the trailhead parking area.

Oso Corredor Trail

See map on page 51

Location: The eastern slope of the Sandias off the Crest Highway; about 30 miles northeast of Albuquerque.

Distance: 8.6-mile loop.

Time: 1 to 2 hours.

Tread: 4.5 miles on singletrack and 4.1 miles on pavement.

Aerobic level: Strenuous. After an initial climb, the singletrack is almost entirely downhill. However, be ready to push on the pavement—a 1,000-foot elevation gain.

Technical difficulty: 3. The challenges are not too bad, especially going down. One technical section rates class 4, followed by Bill Spring Trail, class 2.

Highlights: Oso Corredor, which means "running bear" in Spanish, is one of the newest trails in the system on East Mountain. The year the trail was finished, a drought had driven many bears down into the foothills and may be the reason for the name. Built as a connector trail, Oso Corredor must be reached from either Tree Spring Trail (north) or Bill Spring Trail (south). This loop incorporates both—0.3 mile on Tree Spring Trail and all of Bill Spring Trail, which is smooth and wide, descending along a small creek lined with large oak trees.

Note: Many mountain bikers use Oso Corredor as a northern extension of Faulty Trail.

Land status: Cibola National Forest.

Maps: USGS Sandia Crest and the Forest Service map of Sandia Ranger District.

Access: Travel east from Albuquerque on Interstate 40 for about 15 miles to Exit 175. Take New Mexico 14 north for 6 miles and turn left onto New Mexico 536 (Crest Highway). Park at the trailhead for Tree Spring Trail, which is 5.7 miles up Crest Highway on the left.

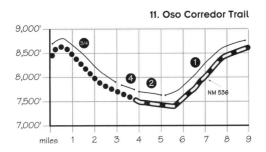

The Ride

0.0 Begin climbing up Tree Spring Trail from the parking area.

0.3 Trail junction. Turn left onto Oso Corredor Trail and gradually descend. Tree Spring Trail continues to 10K Trail at the border of Sandia Mountain Wilderness.

3.3 Oso Corredor joins Faulty Trail. Bear left and down-hill. Encounter some hard, rocky moves and switchbacks as you continue to descend.

3.6 Trail sign indicates Bill Spring Trail. Continue straight. Only a few more technical difficulties and then you can sail down Bill Spring Trail on class 2 terrain.

4.5 Hit pavement and Doc Long Picnic Area. Take the first left and go through the parking area.

4.6 Reach NM 536 and turn left. Climb the paved road back to your car.

8.6 Return to the parking area for Tree Spring Trail.

10K-Ellis Loop

Location: The eastern slope of the Sandias off Crest Highway; about 30 miles northeast of Albuquerque.

Distance: 5-mile loop.

Time: 1 to 2 hours.

Tread: 4 miles on singletrack and 1 mile on pavement.

Aerobic level: Strenuous. Almost half the ride is steady climbing with some steep sections.

Technical difficulty: 3. Good singletrack with some steep, rocky, and narrow terrain. Some of the climbing is on loose rock.

Highlights: This ride combines 10K North Trail with Ellis Trail to create a 5-mile loop. When the trails intersect, both continue into the wilderness area where mountain bikes are not allowed. On 10K North Trail, you will ride mostly downhill through a beautiful dense forest of spruce, fir, and aspen. The excellent wooded singletrack is occasionally interrupted by technical, rocky moves. Once on Ellis Trail, views open to the east down Las Huertas Canyon. This wide trail is the re-

•East Mountain
(Ride 12)

10K North
Trail

Ellis Trail

North Sandia
Peak
10,447'

Media Spring

Ellis Trail

10K North Trail

SANDIA MOUNTAIN
WILDERNESS

536

12

P

TO
14

Sandia
Crest

P

Ellis
Parking Area

N

| 0 | .5 | 1 |

MILES

sult of a 1960s highway construction project that was never completed, due to public protest. The ugly roadcut stretched several miles before it was aborted. Today, wildflowers are plentiful on this meadow-like section of the ride.

Land status: Cibola National Forest.

Maps: USGS Sandia Crest and the national forest map of Sandia Ranger District.

Access: Travel east from Albuquerque on Interstate 40 for about 15 miles to Exit 175. Take New Mexico 14 north for 6 miles and turn left onto New Mexico 536 (Crest Highway). The unimproved dirt parking lot is

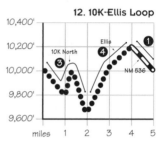

12. 10K-Ellis Loop

11.5 miles up Crest Highway on the right, 2.4 miles past Ninemile Picnic Area.

The Ride

- **0.0** Ride past a small trail sign up into the woods (do not start down the cleared strip) to begin on 10K North Trail, which got its name because it generally follows the 10,000-foot contour line.
- **0.5** At the fork, go right up a short, but very steep ascent. Then enjoy mostly downhill riding for the next 1.5 miles.
- **0.7** Ride under a powerline.
- **1.0** Short 0.1-mile climb.
- **2.0** Trail junction. To the right, a trail leads a short distance into Sandia Mountain Wilderness to Media Spring. Continue the ride left with a short, gradual climb.

2.1 Reach Ellis Trail in an open area, the old road cut. You must go left because of the wilderness boundary. Although the cut is often 100-feet wide, the trail remains mostly singletrack. Begin a section of 15 continuous hills. You'll encounter rocks, downed trees, and rutted sections on your climb.

3.5 Ride under the powerline again.

4.1 Turn left onto Crest Highway and cruise downhill on pavement.

5.0 Arrive back at the parking area.

10K–Tree Spring Loop

Location: The eastern slope of the Sandias off Crest Highway; about 30 miles northeast of Albuquerque.

Distance: 10.8-mile loop.

Time: 1.5 to 2 hours.

Tread: 5.8 miles on singletrack and 5 miles on pavement.

Aerobic level: Strenuous. The singletrack is mostly downhill, but the pavement back to the trailhead climbs continuously.

Technical difficulty: 3. Classic, wooded singletrack broken up occasionally by rocky moves. Sections of Tree Spring Trail rate class 4.

Highlights: The southern half of 10K Trail combined with Tree Spring Trail makes for a great alpine ride. The forest is beautiful at this elevation—spruce, fir, and aspen. 10K South

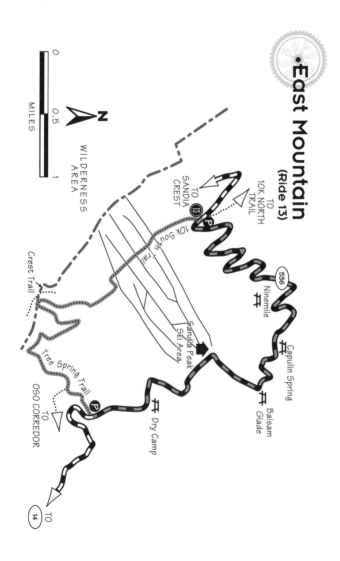

East Mountain
(Ride 13)

MILES
0   0.5   1

N

WILDERNESS AREA

TO SANDIA CREST

TO 10K NORTH TRAIL

10K South Trail

13

P

536
Ninemile

Capulin Spring

Balsam Glade

Sandia Peak Ski Area

Crest Trail

Tree Spring Trail

TO OSO COREDOR

P

Dry Camp

TO 14

Trail begins and ends at 10,000 feet. Good surface and level trail take you across the runs at Sandia Peak Ski Area where the views are spectacular. You'll be losing all your elevation on Tree Spring Trail.

Land status: Cibola National Forest.

Maps: USGS Sandia Crest and the national forest map for Sandia Ranger District.

Access: Travel east from Albuquerque on Interstate 40 for about 15 miles to Exit 175. Take New Mexico 14 north for 6 miles and turn left onto New Mexico 536 (Crest Highway). The unimproved dirt parking lot is 11.5 miles up Crest Highway on the right, 2.4 miles past Ninemile Picnic Area.

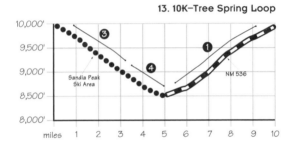

13. 10K–Tree Spring Loop

The Ride

- **0.0** Cross NM 536 and pick up 10K Trail just south (maybe 30 yards) of the parking area. The trail blazes are blue diamonds. Just off the road, keep straight at a trail junction.
- **0.8** Enter Sandia Peak Ski Area. Enjoy good singletrack and good views. Follow the trail closely as you cross the open ski runs.
- **1.5** Leave the ski area boundary.
- **2.6** Reach a trail junction at the edge of the wilderness

area, where mountain bikes are not allowed. Take the sharp left onto Tree Spring Trail and descend steeply.

4.7 Trail junction. The connector trail, Oso Corredor, goes right. (An option for next time?) Continue straight.

5.0 Reach NM 536 and turn left onto pavement. A grueling climb back to the car.

5.5 Pass Dry Camp Picnic Area.

6.3 Reach the base lodge at Sandia Peak Ski Area. Consider riding up King of the Mountain as an alternative to the paved road. Be sure to ask where to pick up 10K Trail.

6.9 Pass Balsam Glade Picnic Area.

7.9 Pass Capulin Spring Picnic Area. Still climbing.

8.3 Pass Ninemile Picnic Area.

10.8 Reach the trailhead parking for 10K Trail.

Sandia Peak Ski Area

King of the Mountain

Location: The eastern slope of the Sandias at Sandia Peak Ski Area; about 30 miles northeast of Albuquerque.

Distance: 16.4 miles out and back.

Time: 2 to 3 hours.

Sandia Crest

(Rides 14-16)

⑮ Upper Tram Terminal
High Finance Restaurant
Observation Deck

⑮

⑮

⑭

AREA BOUNDARY

AREA BOUNDARY

Lift #2

10k Trail

⑮

Lift #1 (Bike Access)

Phone

⑭

Lift #3

⑭

⑭

Pond

⑯

⑯

⑭

Base Lodge

⑭ ⑯

536

TO SANDIA CREST

⑯

TO
⑭

Map courtesy Sandia Peak Ski Company

Tread: 16.4 miles on singletrack.

Aerobic level: Strenuous. As you climb steadily for 8 miles, the chairlift begins to seem like a good idea.

Technical difficulty: 4. Much of the ride is just great singletrack (2 to 3), but be ready for harder challenges such as tight turns, loose rock, extremely narrow trail, and a few unridable sections.

Highlights: King of the Mountain, open for two-way traffic, is rated black by the ski area going up because it is the most difficult trail on the mountain. You will be on Mule Deer and Falcon Ridge for the first 1.6 miles. Check out the ski area's map if this seems confusing. The area is well-marked. For lunch, visit the Double Eagle II Outdoor Grill (at the base), which serves burritos, burgers, and dogs, and a variety of daily specials.

Note: You can take the chairlift up and just ride down King of the Mountain.

Land status: Cibola National Forest.

Maps: USGS Sandia Crest and a map from Sandia Peak Ski Area.

Access: Travel east from Albuquerque on Interstate 40 for about 15 miles to Exit 175. Take New Mexico 14 north for 6 miles and turn left onto New Mexico 536 (Crest Highway). The ski area is about 6 miles up NM 536 on the left.

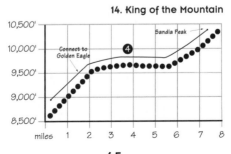

14. King of the Mountain

The Ride

0.0 Leave the lodge, heading right on a dirt road, and ride past the rental shop and ski school buildings.

0.1 Pick up the singletrack on your left at the edge of the ski area.

0.6 A sign indicates Falcon Ridge, right; Bighorn Loop, left. Stay right.

1.6 Climbing a short, steep hill, pass a large pond, and reach a trail junction. You can access Golden Eagle (downhill) by going left. Take the right fork to continue up the mountain. A sign here alerts cyclists about the steep, rocky section ahead.

2.0 How are you doing? Compare your time to Ned's, which is posted here as 11.15 minutes!

2.2 Another trail junction, which accesses Golden Eagle; continue right.

3.0 Reach a sign with three arrows pointing down, warning of a steep descent ahead. There will be several more signs like this during the next 1.5 miles of wooded, rocky singletrack.

4.8 Arrive back out on the open slopes.

8.2 Climb the stairs to reach the observation deck and enjoy the views. On a clear day, the view is fantastic. Then, decide whether to retrace your route down King of the Mountain or pick up Golden Eagle.

16.4 Reach the base of the ski area.

Golden Eagle

See map on page 64

Location: The eastern slope of the Sandias at Sandia Peak Ski Area; about 30 miles northeast of Albuquerque.

Distance: 6.9 miles one-way.

Time: 30 to 45 minutes.

Tread: 6.9 miles on singletrack.

Aerobic level: Easy. It is all downhill. That is what ski area mountain biking is all about, right?

Technical difficulty: 2. You can let gravity have its way; just be ready for some loose rock and tricky switchbacks.

Highlights: Take the chairlift to the top of the mountain and follow Golden Eagle (downhill traffic only) to the base for the ultimate descent. The trail is rated green by the ski area for easiest, but small obstacles, of course, become bigger at high speeds.

High Finance Restaurant and Tavern (at the crest) serves sandwiches, pasta, soup, and salad. Plan on lunch before your ride.

Land status: Cibola National Forest.

Maps: USGS Sandia Crest and a map from Sandia Peak Ski Area.

Access: Travel east from Albuquerque on Interstate 40 for about 15 miles to Exit 175. Take New Mexico 14 north for 6 miles and turn left onto New Mexico 536 (Crest Highway). The ski area is about 6 miles up NM 536 on the left.

15. Golden Eagle

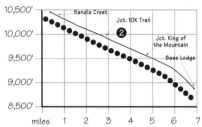

The Ride

0.0 Take the chairlift up and turn left at the top of the mountain to find the trailhead for Golden Eagle.

1.9 Pass a sign indicating King of the Mountain, left; stay right.

3.1 Cross 10K Trail, which is also described in this book.

5.2 Trail junction. The downhill King of the Mountain traffic enters here.

6.9 Reach the base of the ski area.

Lower Mountain Loop

See map on page 64

Location: The eastern slope of the Sandias at Sandia Peak Ski Area; about 30 miles northeast of Albuquerque.

Distance: 3.5-mile loop.

Time: 30 to 45 minutes.

Tread: 3.5 miles on singletrack.

Aerobic level: Moderate. Gentle uphill grade for the first half of the ride.

Technical difficulty: 2 to 3. Fun singletrack with tight turns, loose rock, and super narrow trail.

Highlights: Lower Mountain Loop combines the first leg of King of the Mountain and the last leg of Golden Eagle to create a 3.5-mile loop for bikers who just want a taste of ski area riding. This loop eliminates the technical rocky moves on the upper section of King of the Mountain, but still puts a climb in your ride. The loop is only open one way, counterclockwise, and you don't need to pay for a lift. Bonus!

Land status: Cibola National Forest.

Maps: USGS Sandia Crest and a map from Sandia Peak Ski Area.

Access: Travel east from Albuquerque on Interstate 40 for about 15 miles to Exit 175. Take New Mexico 14 north for 6 miles and turn left onto New Mexico 536 (Crest Highway). The ski area is about 6 miles up NM 536 on the left.

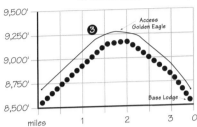

16. Lower Mountain Loop

The Ride

0.0 Leave the lodge, heading right on a dirt road, and ride past the rental shop and ski school buildings.

0.1 Pick up the singletrack trail on your left at the edge of the ski area.

0.6 A sign indicates Falcon Ridge, right; Bighorn Loop, left. Stay right.

1.6 Climb a short, steep hill, pass a large pond, and reach a trail junction. Go left to access Golden Eagle.

1.8 Golden Eagle joins from the right; bear left downhill.

3.5 Reach the base of the ski area.

Northern Slope of the Sandias

Watermelon Trail

Location: The northeastern slope of the Sandias near the town of Placitas; about 25 miles northeast of Albuquerque.

Distance: 15 miles out and back.

Time: 2 to 4 hours.

Tread: 15 miles on dirt road.

Aerobic level: Moderate. The climbing is continuous but gradual for the first half of the ride. But, on the way back down . . . yahoo!

Technical difficulty: 1. This dirt road is obstacle free.

Highlights: Forest Road 16 climbs from just outside the town of Placitas to Balsam Grove Picnic Area on Crest Highway (New Mexico 536). You will follow Las Huertas Creek for most of the ride, pass alongside the limestone cliff bands of Palomas Peak, and as you gain elevation, enjoy spectacular views to the east. Look closely to see the walkway that leads to Sandia Man Cave, a National Historic Landmark and one of most important archeological sites in the country. After your 2,600-foot climb, relax under the ponderosa pines at Balsam Grove Picnic Area and get ready for a fast descent

Northern Slope of the Sandias (Ride 17)

TO
(25)

Placitas

165

(P) (17)

SANDIA MOUNTAIN
WILDERNESS

16

↓↑ (17)

Las Huertas Creek

▲ Sandia Man
Cave

Las Huertas
Picnic Area 🏕

▲ Palomas
Peak
8,685'

Capalin Spring
Picnic Area 🏕 (P)

TO
SANDIA
PEAK

🏕 Balsam Grove
Picnic Area
(P)

536

TO
(14)

N

0   1   2

MILES

back to your car. By the way, *sandia* means watermelon in Spanish.

Note: Use caution descending FR 16 because of occasional car traffic.

Land status: Cibola National Forest.

Maps: The national forest map of Sandia Ranger District and USGS Sandia Crest, Placitas.

Access: Travel north from Albuquerque on Interstate 25 for about 17 miles to Exit 242 and head east on New Mexico 165. You will pass through the town of Placitas after about 6.5 miles. Continue until the road turns to gravel, about 9 miles, and park along the road.

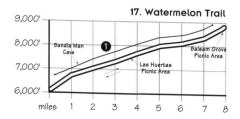

The Ride

0.0 Begin riding up the dirt road; soon you'll be following Las Huertas Creek.

1.2 A pull-off on the left could be used as an alternate starting point.

2.2 Look up to see the cliffside walkway that leads to Sandia Man Cave, then pass the trailhead on the left.

3.9 Las Huertas Picnic Area on the right.

5.0 Randy Road on the right.

6.0 Good views for the next mile.

7.5 Reach pavement at Balsam Grove Picnic Area. Descend via same route to return to your car.

15.0 The ride is complete.

10K Loop Trail

Location: The northern foothills of the Sandias near the town of Placitas; about 20 miles north of Albuquerque.

Distance: 6.2-mile loop.

Time: 30 minutes to 1 hour.

Tread: 6.2 miles on dirt road.

Aerobic level: Easy. A gentle climb during the first 1.5 miles.

Technical difficulty: 1. This dirt road is obstacle free.

Highlights: 10K Loop is basically Forest Road 445. Enjoy good views of the northern Sandias as you ride this graded dirt road. The trail measures exactly 6.2 miles, the length of a 10K, which makes it a convenient training loop for the residents of Placitas. You can access Stripmine Trail from this trailhead or explore several side trails off 10K Loop, which are legal until you reach the wilderness boundary.

Land status: Cibola National Forest.

Maps: The national forest map of Sandia Ranger District and USGS Placitas, Bernalillo.

Access: Travel north from Albuquerque on Interstate 25 for about 17 miles to Exit 242 and head east on New Mexico 165

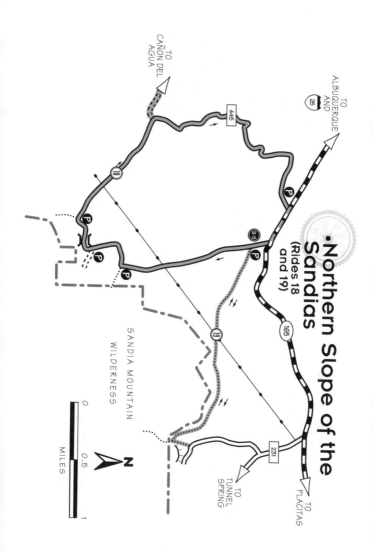

Northern Slope of the Sandias
(Rides 18 and 19)

TO CAÑON DEL AGUA

TO ALBUQUERQUE AND 25

445

18

TO TUNNEL SPRING

TO PLACITAS

231

165

19

SANDIA MOUNTAIN WILDERNESS

N

MILES
0   0.5   1

toward Placitas. After about 3 miles, turn right onto FR 445, located right before mile marker 3. This is the second (or east) entrance to FR 445. (You passed the first one about 0.3 mile back.) Stop at the fee box on the left, pay the fee, then go a short distance to the first parking lot on the left.

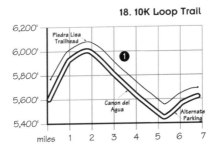

18. 10K Loop Trail

The Ride

0.0 Leave the parking lot heading up FR 445.

0.8 Pass a singletrack trail on the left.

1.4 Pass a large parking lot on the left.

1.8 Continue straight. FR 445A forks left where the Piedra Lisa Trail leads into the Sandia Wilderness Area. Bikes are not allowed.

1.9 Ride across a cattle guard.

2.2 Pass a parking lot with a sign indicating no bikes allowed.

3.4 A road leads off to the left toward Canon del Agua; continue straight.

5.6 Pass a parking lot on the left.

5.7 Pass another fee station near the west entrance of FR 445, then reach paved NM 165 and turn right. You can ride the singletrack that parallels the pavement.

6.0 Turn right onto FR 445, the east entrance.

6.1 Pass the fee station.

6.2 Return to the parking area.

Stripmine Trail

See map on page 75

Location: The northern foothills of the Sandias near the town of Placitas; about 20 miles north of Albuquerque.

Time: 30 to 45 minutes.

Distance: 3.6 miles out and back.

Tread: 3.6 miles on singletrack with short sections of doubletrack.

Aerobic level: Moderate. You will notice a gentle grade for the first half of the ride.

Technical difficulty: 2. Be ready for some loose rocky sections.

Highlights: This short piece of singletrack is on the eastern side of Forest Road 445 (see Ride 18, 10K Loop Trail). You will follow what is left of old mining roads that lead to a small creek and some interesting red cliffs. Early morning light enhances the scenery.

Note: You can create a loop out of this ride by continuing out on the gravel road to Forest Road 231 and returning on paved New Mexico 165. Check the map for details.

Land status: Cibola National Forest.

Maps: The national forest map of Sandia Ranger District and USGS Placitas, Bernalillo.

Access: Travel north from Albuquerque on Interstate 25 for about 17 miles to Exit 242 and head east on NM 165 toward Placitas. After about 3 miles, turn right onto FR 445, located right before mile marker 3. This is the second (or east) entrance to FR 445. (You passed the first one about 0.3 mile back.) Stop at the fee box on the left, pay the fee, then go a short distance to the first parking lot on the left.

19. Stripmine Trail

The Ride

0.0 Leave the parking area on singletrack through an opening in a fence.

0.1 Ride through a small, dry wash. Continue straight when a doubletrack trail comes in from the right.

0.9 Watch for a steep drop-off to the left of the trail. Begin riding parallel to a large, dry wash.

1.6 Reach a fork, go left, and soon cross a creek. (The hard left also leads to the creek and brings you back to the main trail.)

1.7 Be sure to take the side trail on the right, which leads to some interesting rock formations. Great picnic spot.

1.8 Reach a fence at the border of a subdivision of Placitas. You can ride out the gravel road and back on NM 165 or turn around and retrace your route to the trailhead.

3.6 Return to FR 445.

The Foothills

North Foothills Trail

Location: The foothills of the Sandias at the eastern edge of Albuquerque.

Distance: 10-mile loop.

Time: 1 to 2 hours.

Tread: 10 miles on singletrack.

Aerobic level: Moderate. Rolling with several gradual climbs.

Technical difficulty: 3. Has short rocky sections and soft sand, plus several hard (possibly unridable) moves into and out of streambeds.

Highlights: The Foothills Trail System, which borders the Sandia Mountain Wilderness, is the result of the hard work of many individuals and organizations. Albuquerque Open Space, along with the Forest Service, secured a large portion of the western foothills of the Sandias to be preserved as a multi-use area. In addition to this trail, the system includes South Foothills Trail, a few miles south of Embudito. Both areas offer an up-close look at the rugged granite peaks of the Sandias, as well as views west of the city and the Rio Grande Valley. You'll ride through juniper and pinyon and interesting large boulder fields. The Foothills Trail System is extremely popular due to the good riding conditions and its close proximity to the city.

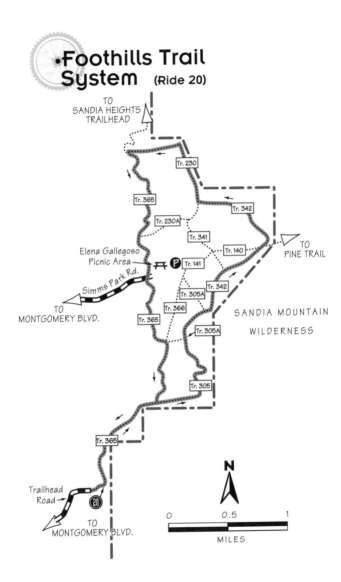

Foothills Trail System (Ride 20)

TO SANDIA HEIGHTS TRAILHEAD

Tr. 230

Tr. 342

Tr. 365

Tr. 230A

Tr. 341

Tr. 140

TO PINE TRAIL

Elena Gallegoso Picnic Area

Tr. 141

Simms Park Rd.

TO MONTGOMERY BLVD.

Tr. 342

Tr. 305A

Tr. 366

SANDIA MOUNTAIN

Tr. 365

WILDERNESS

Tr. 305A

Tr. 305

Tr. 365

Trailhead Road

20

TO MONTGOMERY BLVD.

N

0   0.5   1

MILES

Expect the trails to be crowded during peak hours and on weekends. Much of the singletrack is hard-packed and smooth so you can ride fast except for a few climbs. Be prepared for some wet crossings in the spring. Once you try this loop, consult the map to create your own route using the alternate side trails. You can ride here year-round. Elena Gallegos Picnic Area, located in the center of this network of trails, provides picnic tables, grills, and restrooms, but you must pay a parking fee of $1 on weekdays and $2 on weekends. The picnic area is open from 7 A.M. to 7 P.M. in the winter and from 7 A.M. to 9 P.M. in the summer. Annual parking passes are available from the Open Space Division. Travel north of Montgomery Boulevard on Tramway Boulevard for 2 miles to access this city recreational facility. Make a right turn and follow the signs.

Land status: Cibola National Forest and Albuquerque Open Space.

Maps: A map from Albuquerque Open Space and USGS Sandia Crest, Tijeras.

Access: Travel about 3 miles north from Albuquerque on Interstate 25 to Exit 228 and take Montgomery Boulevard east toward the Sandias. After about 6.5 miles, reach the traffic light at Tramway Boulevard. Continue straight through this intersection for 0.5 mile to a four-way stop. Turn left onto Glenwood Hills Road, travel another 0.5 mile, and turn right onto Trailhead Road. Drive 0.2 mile to Embudito Trailhead. The parking area is open from 7 A.M. to 10 P.M.

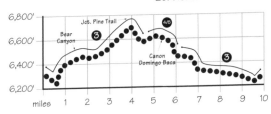

The Ride

- **0.0** Head north on the singletrack to the left of the information board. A short distance into the ride, veer left at the fork.
- **1.1** Veer right onto Trail 305.
- **1.9** Cross Bear Canyon Arroyo.
- **2.2** Cross a gravel road.
- **2.5** Stay right. Trail 305A goes left to intersect with Trail 365.
- **3.0** Another junction with Trail 305A left; continue straight.
- **3.3** At the fork, go right onto Trail 342. Trail 341 leads into the picnic area.
- **3.8** Large information board and intersection with Pino Trail 140. Bikers are not allowed on this trail. Continue straight, cross an arroyo, and begin a fun descent.
- **4.4** Good view of Albuquerque's aerial tramway.
- **4.7** Reach Trail 230, turn right, and begin a rocky climb. This section is the most technical part of the ride.
- **5.2** Be careful. Double drops before crossing Canon de Domingo Baca may force you to dismount. A technical climb follows.
- **5.8** Reach Trail 365 and turn left. (For more mileage and worthwhile riding, turn right and head north toward

the Sandia Heights Trailhead near the Lower Tramway Terminal. Out-and-back adds 2.8 miles.)

7.3 Cross paved Simms Park Road, which leads into Elena Gallegos Picnic Area.

8.1 Confusing intersection; stay right.

8.9 Return to the beginning of the loop, continue straight, retracing the first 1.1 miles of the ride.

10.0 End of ride.

South Foothills Trail

Location: The foothills of the Sandias at the eastern edge of Albuquerque.

Distance: 6-mile loop.

Time: 30 minutes to 1 hour.

Tread: 5.5 miles on singletrack and 0.5 mile on doubletrack.

Aerobic level: Moderate. You will find a few more climbs here than on North Foothills Trail. The half-mile climb at mile 2.7 will get your heart pumping.

Technical difficulty: 2 to 3. The backside of U Mound might force you out of the saddle.

Highlights: South Foothills Trail, like its sister to the north, is part of the Foothills Trail System. For more specifics on this multi-use area, see Ride 20, North Foothills Trail. This area is less developed and may seem like a spiderweb of trails at first, but the loop is fairly easy to follow. Plans are in the works to

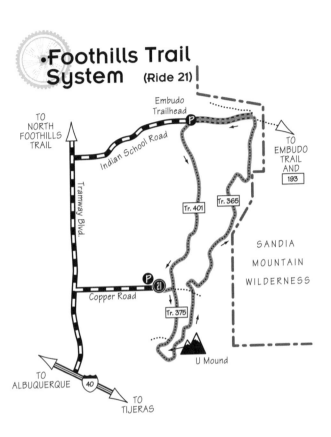

Foothills Trail System (Ride 21)

TO
NORTH
FOOTHILLS
TRAIL

Embudo
Trailhead

Indian School Road

Tramway Blvd.

TO
EMBUDO
TRAIL
AND
193

Tr. 401

Tr. 365

SANDIA

MOUNTAIN

WILDERNESS

P 21

Copper Road

Tr. 375

U Mound

TO
ALBUQUERQUE

40

TO
TIJERAS

N

0   0.5   1

MILES

put up better trail markers and eliminate confusing side trails. This ride is less crowded than North Foothills Trail and the steep switchbacks are worth the visit. Much of the loop is smooth, hard-packed singletrack. Ride fast!

Note: You can bypass the U Mound, a small mountain in the second half-mile, by hanging a left as you approach it. The backside is narrow and rocky.

Land status: Cibola National Forest and Albuquerque Open Space.

Maps: USGS Tijeras and a map from Albuquerque Open Space.

Access: Travel east from Albuquerque on Interstate 40 for about 8 miles to Exit 167 and follow Tramway Boulevard north for 0.7 mile to Copper Road. Turn right and drive to the terminus of Copper Road at a paved parking area, which is open from 7 A.M. to 10 P.M.

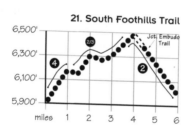

21. South Foothills Trail

The Ride

0.0 Head straight ahead out of the parking lot on Trail 400. Reach a marker for Trail 375 and turn right.

0.5 Confusing trail junction. Take the right trail that goes up the west side of a small mountain. You may have to walk the technical backside.

0.8 After a steep 0.1-mile descent, take the trail to the right along the base of the Sandias.

1.5 Cross Trail 400 and begin a short, steep climb on switchbacks.

1.7 Go right and descend.

2.2 At a trail sign indicating the direction of Copper and Embudo Trailheads, continue straight.

2.7 Cross a large arroyo and begin another climb on switchbacks.

3.1 Reach a high point at a confusing trail junction. Take the trail straight ahead that leads across a small bridge.

3.7 Reach a fork, go left onto Trail 193, and descend on doubletrack.

4.2 Large parking lot at Embudo Trailhead. Locate the singletrack on the left across from the information board. Keep right and soon you'll be riding along a fence. (For the next 2 miles, stay right at any trail junctions. This should keep you on Trail 401.)

5.9 Intersect Trail 400 and turn right.

6.0 Return to the parking lot.

Along the Rio Grande

Corrales Bosque

Location: Along the Rio Grande near the town of Corrales; about 10 miles north of Albuquerque.

Distance: 14.4 miles out and back.

Time: 1.5 to 2 hours.

Tread: 13.8 miles on singletrack and 0.6 mile on pavement. Occasionally, you will come out of the bosque and ride on the ditch road for a short distance.

Aerobic level: Easy. No significant elevation change.

Technical difficulty: 2. The smooth, hard-packed singletrack is occasionally interrupted with sections of bumpy tread from horse traffic, some soft sand, and a couple of log jumps.

Highlights: A perfect ride for a lazy winter afternoon. You will travel through part of the Rio Grande bosque, a special habitat located in the floodplain of the river. This lush woodland contains one of the largest cottonwood forests in the country—quite a contrast to the surrounding desert environment. To learn more about the bosque, visit the Rio Grande Nature Center just west of the intersection of Candelaria and Rio Grande Boulevard. As you parallel the river, enjoy views east toward the Sandias, and keep your eyes peeled for migratory waterfowl, especially between November and February.

Along the Rio Grande

(Ride 22)

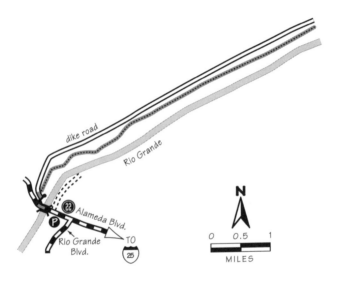

dike road

Rio Grande

22 Alameda Blvd.

P

Rio Grande
Blvd.

TO

25

N

0   0.5   1

MILES

In addition to the dominant cottonwoods, this riverside forest includes box elders, willows, and many shrubs, grasses, and wildflowers.

Land status: Rio Grande Valley State Park, Albuquerque Open Space, and The Nature Conservancy.

Maps: USGS Alameda, Bernalillo, and Los Griegos.

Access: Travel north from Albuquerque on Interstate 25 for about 7 miles to Exit 233 (Alameda Boulevard). Head west on Alameda for about 3.5 miles. After crossing South Rio Grande Boulevard, turn left into a large parking lot marked with a brown sign "Alameda/Rio Grande Open Space." The parking lot is closed from 9 P.M. to 7 A.M.

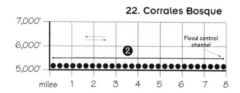

The Ride

0.0 Take a right out of the parking lot on the paved path and go under Alameda Boulevard. Then take the small bridge on the left across a clear ditch.

0.1 Ride across the Rio Grande on a large bridge.

0.3 Take a right through the red gate to access the ditch road.

0.4 Look down to the right to locate the singletrack.

0.6 After you ride between the ditch and some metal fencing, ignore the trail on the right and continue straight.

1.0	Reach a ramp for the ditch and turn right, then take the next trail to the left.
1.4	Ride over a ramp and along the ditch, then back in the bosque.
2.9	First nice river access.
3.6	Reach another ramp to the ditch and veer right toward the river.
3.7	Good river access; ride through the first of a dozen or so metal fences in the next mile. Some of the fences will force you off the bike because of a low cable. This section has great winter views of the Sandias.
4.7	Ride through the last of the metal fences.
4.9	River access with a nice beach.
6.8	River access with a rope swing.
6.9	After a ramp to the ditch, turn right and head for the river.
7.0	Enjoy riding close to the banks of the Rio Grande.
7.1	Parallel the ditch for a short distance.
7.2	Trail's end. Reach a break in the bosque and a flood control channel. Take the side trail to the right for one last view of the Rio Grande and Sandia Crest before returning via the same route.
14.4	Reach the parking area on Alameda.

South Valley Canal Road

Location: Along the Rio Grande; about 5 miles south of Albuquerque.

Distance: 10 miles out and back with several additional miles possible.

Time: 1 to 1.5 hours.

Tread: 7.2 miles on doubletrack and 2.8 miles on pavement. The additional miles are doubletrack.

Aerobic level: Easy. No significant elevation change.

Technical difficulty: 1. This dirt road has some bumpy tread and soft sand.

Highlights: South Valley Canal Road is the quickest way to get out of the city and explore the countryside, although most mountain bikers would consider this ride boring. You won't ride alongside the river or through the cottonwoods like at Corrales Bosque; rather, you will parallel the clear ditch and can still enjoy the shade (afternoon), the waterfowl (winter is best), and the views east toward the Sandias (on the way back). The Rio Grande Valley State Park runs for 25 miles along both sides of the river from Sandia Pueblo to Isleta Pueblo. The main goal of the park is to preserve the special habitat called a bosqud, which is located in the floodplain of the river. For more information on this unique environment, see Ride 22, Corrales Bosque, which is also part of the state park.

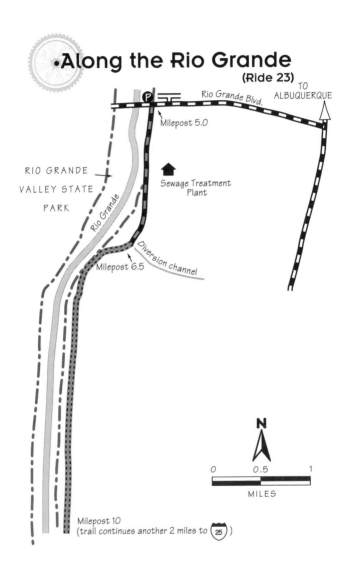

•Along the Rio Grande
(Ride 23)

P
Rio Grande Blvd.
TO ALBUQUERQUE

Milepost 5.0

RIO GRANDE
VALLEY STATE
PARK

Rio Grande

Sewage Treatment
Plant

Diversion channel

Milepost 6.5

N

0   0.5   1
MILES

Milepost 10
(trail continues another 2 miles to 25)

Note: This ride is just one of several access points to the dirt and paved trails in the park. Albuquerque Open Space puts out a trail map of the entire area.

Land status: Rio Grande Valley State Park, Albuquerque Open Space, and The Nature Conservancy.

Maps: USGS Albuquerque West, and Isleta; and the Rio Grande Valley State Park Trail Map, available from Albuquerque Open Space.

Access: Travel south from Albuquerque on Interstate 25 for about 5 miles to Exit 220 (Rio Bravo Boulevard). Head west (right) on Rio Bravo for about 1.5 miles. Just before the bridge over the Rio Grande, turn right onto Poco Loco, then immediately turn left. The parking lot is at the end of this road.

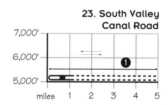

23. South Valley
Canal Road

The Ride

0.0 Leave the parking area and ride under Rio Bravo Boulevard to access the paved trail alongside the clear ditch.

0.3 Ride over a wooden bridge.

0.7 Pass a sewage treatment plant. The scenery gets better than this!

1.4 After riding over another wooden bridge, bear right on the dirt road, then head left over the cement diversion channel. On the other side, pick up the canal road near the Open Space milepost marker "6.5 miles."

2.5 Pass several large ranches.

3.5 Begin riding alongside open pasture land.

5.0 Reach milepost marker "10 miles." You can keep riding as far as I-25, about milepost 12, if you want. The scenery continues to improve the farther south into the valley you go.

10.0 Return to the parking area on Rio Bravo Boulevard.

Petroglyph National Monument

Volcanoes North

Location: On West Mesa; about 15 miles west of Albuquerque.

Distance: 7.2-mile loop.

Time: 1 to 1.5 hours.

Tread: 5.2 miles on doubletrack and 2 miles on dirt road.

Petroglyph National Monument

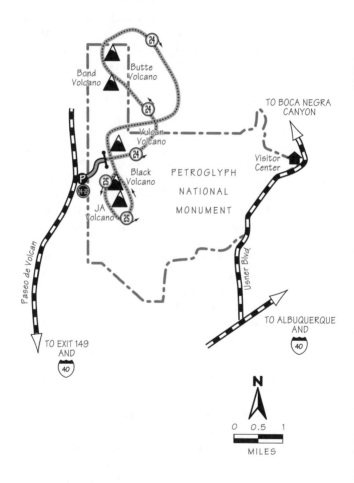

Bond Volcano

Butte Volcano

Vulcan Volcano

Black Volcano

JA Volcano

PETROGLYPH

NATIONAL

MONUMENT

TO BOCA NEGRA CANYON

Visitor Center

Paseo de Volcan

Usner Blvd.

TO EXIT 149 AND 40

TO ALBUQUERQUE AND 40

N

0   0.5   1

MILES

Aerobic level: Moderate. A few of the climbs are steep but short.

Technical difficulty: 2. The loose, rocky terrain, especially on the climbs, might make this ride seem a bit harder.

Highlights: Look toward Albuquerque's western horizon and you will see the distinctive volcano cones on West Mesa, which erupted about 110,000 years ago. The area is part of Petroglyph National Monument and offers mountain bikers some fun exploring on old dirt roads. While it may be hard to follow the directions in this book, it is nearly impossible to get lost out there. Just take whatever trail looks interesting and keep your eyes on the volcanoes. You will ride through open grassland with sagebrush, yucca, prickly pear, cholla, and saltbush. Sections of trail narrow to singletrack and several climbs have technical moves. I highly recommend a late afternoon ride. Highlights include views of the city lights and spectacular sunsets over Mount Taylor. If possible, take a ride out to the mesa during the famous Albuquerque Balloon Fiesta and enjoy a great vantage point.

Petroglyph National Monument is known for its prehistoric rock art, some 15,000 images scratched on the basalt rocks. These symbols had spiritual and cultural significance to the early inhabitants along the Rio Grande. To learn more, check out the visitor center off Interstate 40, 3 miles north on Usner Boulevard. (Open year-round from 8 A.M. to 5 P.M. except Thanksgiving, Christmas, and New Year's Day.)

Land status: Petroglyph National Monument and Albuquerque Open Space.

Maps: USGS Los Griegos and The Volcanoes.

Access: Travel west from Albuquerque on I-40 for 9 miles to Exit 149. Go north on Paseo Del Volcano Boulevard toward Double Eagle Airport for about 4.5 miles and turn right into a dirt parking lot marked with a sign "Petroglyph National Monument."

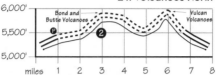

24. Volcanoes North

The Ride

- **0.0** Begin riding the dirt road around the gate toward the volcanoes.
- **1.0** Reach a second lot, which can be used as alternate parking if you want to avoid the dirt road. (Be sure you will be out by 5 P.M. when the gate closes.) Go inside the fence and take the middle trail, which heads northeast.
- **1.2** Take the right fork.
- **1.5** Take the left fork.
- **2.5** At the crossroads, go straight under the powerlines and head up the eastern side of Bond Volcano.
- **3.3** Reach the top of Butte Volcano and be ready for a steep, rocky downhill.
- **3.4** At the T intersection, turn right and ride along the powerline for 0.5 mile.
- **4.1** Turn right, leaving the trail under the powerline and heading west.
- **4.7** Return to the crossroads near the initial powerlines (mile 2.5), and continue straight.
- **5.7** Reach a high point on the backside of Vulcan Volcano. A trail leads left; continue straight and around the south side of the volcano.
- **6.0** Bear right downhill toward the second parking lot.
- **6.2** Return to the second parking lot and ride the dirt road back to your vehicle.
- **7.2** End of ride.

Volcanoes South

See map on page 95

Location: On West Mesa; about 15 miles west of Albuquerque.

Distance: 4-mile loop.

Time: 30 to 45 minutes.

Tread: 2 miles on doubletrack and 2 miles on dirt road.

Aerobic level: Easy. The climbs are more gradual than Volcanoes North, Ride 24.

Technical difficulty: 2. The loose, rocky terrain, especially on the climbs, might make this ride seem a bit harder.

Highlights: This is the easier of the two loops at Petroglyph National Monument. It is worth riding the loops together as a big "figure 8."

The area is part of Petroglyph National Monument and offers mountain bikers some fun exploring on old dirt roads. While it may be hard to follow the directions in this book, it is nearly impossible to get lost out there. Just take whatever trail looks interesting and keep your eyes on the volcanoes. You will ride through open grassland with sagebrush, yucca, prickly pear, cholla, and saltbush. Sections of trail narrow to singletrack and several climbs have technical moves. I highly recommend a late afternoon ride. Highlights include views of the city lights and spectacular sunsets over Mount Taylor. If possible, take a ride out to the mesa during the famous Albuquerque International Balloon Fiesta and enjoy a great vantage point. Petroglyph National Monument is known for its prehistoric rock art, some 15,000 images scratched on the basalt rocks. These symbols had spiritual and cultural significance to the early inhabitants along the Rio Grande. To learn more, check out the visitor center off Interstate 40, 3 miles north on Usner Boulevard. (Open year-round from 8 A.M. to 5 P.M. except Thanksgiving, Christmas, and New Year's Day.)

Land status: Petroglyph National Monument and Albuquerque Open Space.

Maps: USGS Los Griegos and The Volcanoes.

Access: Travel west from Albuquerque on I-40 for 9 miles to Exit 149. Go north on Paseo Del Volcano Boulevard toward Double Eagle Airport for about 4.5 miles and turn right into a dirt parking lot marked with a sign "Petroglyph National Monument."

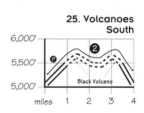

The Ride

0.0 Begin riding the dirt road around the gate toward the volcanoes.

1.0 Reach a second parking lot, which can be used as an alternate starting point if you want to avoid the dirt road. (Be sure you will be out by 5 P.M. when the gate closes.) Go inside the fence and ride south along the fence to begin this loop.

1.1 Ride up and over the eastern side of Black Volcano.

1.2 Take the right fork.

1.6 At the crossroads, continue straight.

1.8 Begin circling around JA Volcano. At the southern-most point, go right away from the volcano, then left at the next trail to continue around.

2.4 A trail comes in from the left, which leads back to the crossroads at mile 1.6. Continue straight.

2.8 Reach the junction where the trail forked at mile 1.2. Continue straight.

3.0 Return to the alternate parking lot and head back out the dirt road to your vehicle.

4.0 End of ride.

Appendix A

Resources

Albuquerque Chamber of Commerce
P.O. Box 25100
Albuquerque, NM 87125
(505) 764-3700

Albuquerque Convention and Visitor's Bureau
P.O. Box 26866
625 Silver Avenue SW
Albuquerque, NM 87125
(505) 243-3696
(800) 284-2282

Albuquerque Open Space Division
P.O. Box 1293
Albuquerque, NM 87103
(505) 873-6620

Bureau of Land Management
Albuquerque District Office
435 Montano Road NE
Albuquerque, NM 87107
(505) 761-8700

Cibola National Forest
Main Headquarters
2113 Osuna Road, Suite A
Albuquerque, NM 87713-1001
(505) 761-4650

Cibola National Forest
Sandia Ranger District
11776 Highway 337
Tijeras, NM 87059-8619
(505) 281-3304

Cibola National Forest
Mountainair Ranger District
P.O. Box 69
Mountainair, NM 87036
(505) 847-2990

East Mountain Chamber of Commerce
P.O. Box 765
Cedar Crest, NM 87008
(505) 281-5099

Petrogylph National Monument
6001 Unser Boulevard NW
Albuquerque, NM 87120
(505) 899-0205

Rio Grande Nature Center State Park
2901 Candelaria Road NW
Albuquerque, NM 87107
(505) 344-7240

Sandia Peak Ski and Tramway
10 Tramway Loop NE
Albuquerque, NM 87122
(505) 242-2540

Two Wheel Drive bicycle shop
Charles G. Ervin, president
1706 Central Avenue SE
Albuquerque, NM 87106
(505) 243-8443

Appendix B

Bike Shops

Albuquerque Bikes
2641 San Mateo NE
(505) 888-3730 (Three locations)

Bike City
1130 Juan Tabo NE
(505) 293-2888

Bike Coop
3407 Central NE
(505) 265-5170

Bike World
1820 Central SE
(505) 247-8033 (Two locations)

Campus Bicycles
106 Vassar Drive SE
(505) 268-6547

Cycle Cave
5716 Menual Boulevard NE
(505) 884-6607

Cycle Source
2520 San Mateo
(505) 883-7399

Fat Tire Cycles
1425 Central NE
(505) 243-5900

Northeast Cyclery
8305 Menual Boulevard NE
(505) 299-1210 (Two locations, rentals)

Old Town Bicycles
2209-B Central NW
(505) 247-4926

R.E.I
1905 Mountain Road NW
(505) 247-1191

Rio Mountain Sport
1210 Rio Grande NW
(505) 766-9970 (Rentals)

Ski Systems
1605 Juan Tabo NE
(505) 296-9111

Sportz Outdoor
6950 Montgomery Boulevard NE (505) 837-9400

Two Wheel Drive bicycle shop
1706 Central SE
(505) 243-8443

World Championship Bicycles
300 Yale Boulevard SE
(505) 268-5697

In addition, Sandia Peak Ski Area offers a full-service bike shop, and suspension bikes can be rented at the top or bottom of the mountain. At the base of East Mountain, right where Sandia Crest Highway joins with New Mexico 14, you will find a small bike shop that also sells snowboards and brew supplies.

A Short Index of Rides

About the Author

After ten years living and working on the Chattooga River in South Carolina, Nicole Blouin moved to the Southwest. With the manuscript for *Mountain Biking South Carolina* finished, she spent the next year riding the trails around Albuquerque and teaching at the Santa Fe Climbing Gym. *Mountain Biking Albuquerque* is her fourth book.